Beginner's Guide to Google Apps Script Sheets & Forms Book 1 & 2

by

Barrie Roberts

Contents

Introduction 7
   What is Google Apps Script? 7
   Why use Google Apps Script? 8
   Example files and full pieces of code 8

CHAPTER 1 – First Script 13
   First Google Apps Script 13
   Methods 17
   Renaming a project 21
   Authorizing a script 21

CHAPTER 2 – Variables and getting & setting values 25
     The Code 26

CHAPTER 3 – Loops 33
   Loop 1 – Print "Hello!" 20 times down column A 34
   Loop 2 – Print numbers 1 to 20 down column A 37
   Loop 3 – Fill cells A1 to A20 in blue 38
   Loop 4 – Fill cells A1 to A20 in blue and print numbers 1 to 20 39
   Loop 5 – Print the numbers 1 to 20 across 10 different columns 41
   Loop 6 – Create 5 documents and name them Document1 to Document5 43
   Loop 7 – Create 4 documents each with names from the sheet 44
   Scope 45

CHAPTER 4 – Arrays, Log & Executions 48
   Introducing the Execution log 48
   Single items and multiple items 50
   Accessing values in arrays 51
   Using getValues() and setValues() to get a range of values in one go 53
   How arrays relate to rows and columns on a spreadsheet 55
   Looping through an array 56
   Setting up an empty array and adding to it 57
   Reducing the execution time 60

CHAPTER 5 – If, Prompt, Menu & OnOpen Trigger 62
   Creating new script file 62
   Create a new spreadsheet menu 64
   If statements (conditionals) 65

Example 1 – Set the background to red if the attendance is <80%... 65

Example 2 – Set the background to red if the attendance is <80% or otherwise green 67

Example 3 – Set the background to red if the attendance is <70%, yellow 70-80%, green 80% or more.. 68

Example 4 – Set the background to red if the attendance is <80% OR the exam mark is <70% 69

Example 5 – Set the background to green if the attendance is 80% or more AND the exam mark is 70% or more 71

Example 6 – Get the students' data and add it to their individual sheet 72

Example 6B – Return back to the first sheet.. 74

Example 7 – Ask for the student's name, then open their individual sheet... 75

Example 8 – Set the background to red if the attendance is <80% otherwise green (ternary operator) .. 76

Example 9 – Set the background colour for all students' attendance figures 78

CHAPTER 6 – SpreadsheetApp & the For In Loop 81

Google Workspace Services 81

Spreadsheet Service 82

SpreadsheetApp 83

Creating menu – SpreadsheetApp.getUi()... 86

Global Variables / variables 87

Example 1 – Creating a new spreadsheet.. 88

Example 2 – Creating a spreadsheet with limited rows and columns... 88

Example 3 – Creating a spreadsheet with a name from the sheet 90

Example 4 – Creating multiple spreadsheets with different names 90

Example 5 – Getting data from one spreadsheet and adding it to another (URL)................................... 92

Example 6 – Getting data from one spreadsheet and adding it to another (ID)...................................... 93

Example 7 – Creating multiple spreadsheets with different names and different pieces of text............. 94

CHAPTER 7 – Spreadsheet Class 96

Example 1 – Copying and renaming a spreadsheet and using the Toast message 97

Example 2 – Adding editors or viewers to a spreadsheet... 98

Example 3 – Moving a sheet to a new location 100

Example 4 – Moving a sheet to a new location using getNumSheets()... 101

Example 5 – Inserting and deleting sheets 102

CHAPTER 8 – Sheet Class 104

Example 1 – Copying a hidden master sheet and renaming it.. 105

Example 2 – Hiding and inserting rows and columns 107

Example 3 – Appending a name to a list and sorting it alphabetically 110

Example 4 – Extracting data from a table and creating a new sheet with that data 111

Example 5 – Extracting data from a table and creating a new sheet with that data (Quicker method) .. 115

CHAPTER 9 – Range class & Triggers 118

Example 1 – On opening a spreadsheet, highlight a specific cell & clear its content 118

Example 2 – Add a formula to a cell when a form is submitted 120

Example 3 – Add a formula when a form is submitted and format the responses............................ 123

Example 4 – Change cell colour when a specific cell is edited, using onEdit().. 125

Example 5 – Highlight whole row when a cell is edited 128

Example 6 – Sort table by multiple columns.. 130

Example 7 – Copy part of a table to a new sheet.. 131

CHAPTER 10: First Forms script.. 139

First Google Forms script 139

CHAPTER 11: Creating & updating a Google Form... 143

Example 1 - Creating a Form with a multiple-choice question 143

Example 2 - Creating a Form with data from a Google Sheet... 145

Example 3 - Updating a question in a Form from data in a Google Sheet...................................... 147

CHAPTER 12: Creating & updating a multiple question Form... 150

Example 1 - Creating multiple questions in a Google Form... 150

Example 2 - Updating multiple questions in a Google Form.. 154

CHAPTER 13: Adding different types of questions to a form 158

Overview of script 158

Creating a new Google Form... 159

Getting the data from the sheet 159

Looping down the rows of questions 160

Checking the question type 160

    Functions to make the questions 161

    Making a text question 161

    Making a date question 162

    Making a duration question... 162

    Making a multiple-choice question 163

    Making a list question.. 165

    Making a scale question 165

    Making a checkbox question 167

    Making a grid question 167

    Making a paragraph question 169

Further information 172

CHAPTER 14: Using Form responses 173

Example 1a - Problem-reporting log & email (Sheet version) 173

    The Code 174

Example 1b - Problem-reporting log & email (Form version) 177

    The Code 178

Example 2 - Move students' pieces of writing to their individual sheets 180

    The Code 181

Example 3 - Appointment System 182

    The Code 183

CHAPTER 15: Form validation 188

Clocking in & out form 188

The Code 188

Other validations 192

CHAPTER 16: Form page navigation 194

The Code 195

    Clocking in form - Page 1 195

    Clocking in form - Page 2 196

    Clocking in form - Page 3 198

    Clocking in form - Page 4 198

CHAPTER 17: Making quizzes in Forms 204

The Code 204

Further Reading 213

Apps Script Websites 215

About the author 220

Appendix 1 – Files and Code from each chapter 222

Chapter 1 – First Script 222

Chapter 2 – Variables and Getting & Setting Values 222

Chapter 3 – Loops 223

Chapter 4 – Arrays, Log & Executions 224

Chapter 5 – If, Prompt, Menu & OnOpen Trigger 226

Chapter 6 – SpreadsheetApp and for in loop 230

Chapter 7 – Spreadsheet 232

Chapter 8 - Sheet 233

    Chapter 9 – Range 235

Appendix 2 – Files and code from each chapter (Forms) 238

    Chapter 10 – First Form Script 238

    Chapter 11 – Creating & updating a Google Form 238

        Example 1.. 238

        Example 2.. 238

        Example 3.. 238

    Chapter 12 – Creating & updating a multiple question Form 239

        Example 1.. 239

        Example 2.. 239

    Chapter 13 – Adding different types of questions to a Form 240

    Chapter 14 – Using Form responses 243

        Example 1 - Problem log 243

        Example 2 - Assignments 244

        Example 3 - Appointments 245

    Chapter 15 - Form validation 246

    Chapter 16 – Form page navigation 246

    Chapter 17 – Making quizzes in Google Forms 248

Appendix 3 – Script Editor and creating a standalone script 249

    Tour of the Script editor 249

    Overview 250

    Editor 251

    Helpful Editor tools 252

        Formatting (indenting) your document... 252

        Highlighting all positions of a variable... 253

        Highlighting pairs of brackets 253

        Hiding blocks of code 253

        Find where a variable is defined 254

    Triggers 254

    Executions 256

    Project settings 257

    Sharing and help 258

    Files, Libraries, and Services... 258

    Creating a standalone Apps Script file... 260

Introduction

The idea of this book is to introduce you to the wonderful world of Google Apps Script (GAS). It assumes you have no previous coding knowledge and all the examples take you step-by-step, explaining the code as we go. I'll also cover some JavaScript basics and these are in the context of Apps Script, as I've found that a lot of JavaScript examples and tutorials on-line, only talk about its use with web pages.

Why did I write this book?

When I first started learning the language, I didn't know what I was doing and I fumbled my way through various examples on-line, learning by trial and error, and what struck me was that even though you can search for a specific answer to something, there was very little out there in terms of learning Apps Script in a more course kind of way, where it goes from the basics to more complex codes, and where the code is explained to you.

So, that's the idea of this book, I want you to go from knowing nothing, to being able to create some cool, useful pieces of code and know how they were put together, to enable you to write your own pieces of code for your own situations. I'm assuming you have a base knowledge of Google Sheets and Forms, in particular, how to create new sheets and navigate around them. If not, then I would recommend reading my books on Sheets and Forms. See the *About the author* section.

What is Google Apps Script?

Google Apps Script is a scripting language based on JavaScript that sits behind a number of the Google Workspace products, such as Google Docs, Google Forms, and Google Sheets. It is cloud-based and so all your scripts live on the Google servers, not locally or your computer, allowing you access to them the same way you can access the Google Workspace products and services.

The main App services you can use Apps Script with are:

Calendar, Contacts, Docs, Drive, Forms, Gmail, Groups, Translate, Maps, Sites, Sheets

There are more but this book will focus on **Sheets** and **Forms**, as I feel these are both the easiest and the most useful ones to start with.

Why use Google Apps Script?

There are three main reasons why you would want to use GAS.

1. Automating tasks – It's particularly useful for repetitive tasks, which can save you a lot of time. You can set up a menu where at a click of a button the program does what you would have had to do manually. It also ensures those tasks are done well. What I mean here is that the program will carry out the same instructions exactly every time, whereas a human might make mistakes or they may do it in their own way.

2. Extending the functionality of the Google Workspace products and services – This allows you to do far more than what's in the current products, making the products more suited to your specific needs. A good example of this, are the add-ons you can download for some of the Google Workspace products, which add extra functionality to the original product.

3. Connecting the products together – The beauty of GAS is that the various products and services can all be connected together, and you're not just confined to using one product at a time. This book is focused on the use with Google Sheets and Google Forms, and you will see how the Forms can use data from Sheets and vice versa. Later in the book, you'll also find examples where we also use services like Mail, to send automatic emails based on Form submissions that are stored in a Google Sheet.

Example files and full pieces of code

Links to all the files and full pieces of code used in this book can be found in Appendix 1 and 2. I thoroughly recommend using the files that go with this book, as they will help you understand how the code works in situ and allow you to play with it and adapt it.

This book is a combination of two books, one focused on Google Sheets and the other on Google Forms, although as you'll see when you start using Apps Script that you will use the different services together.

GOOGLE SHEETS

Apps Script with Google Sheets

If you're just starting out, I recommend starting off in Sheets, as personally, I found it the easiest to get my head around how Apps Script works and the sheet and cell structure of a spreadsheet is easier to understand.

What am I going to learn in this part of the book?

As you go through this book, I will introduce you to new parts of Apps Script (mainly methods) and also introduce you to key concepts in JavaScript and their associated code. So, every chapter will build on previous ones.

Chapter	Apps Script classes and methods	JavaScript concepts
1	SpreadsheetApp() getActiveSpreadsheet() getActiveSheet() getRange() setValue()	Functions
2	getValues() setValues() setBackground() setFontWeight() setHorizontalAlignment()	Variables - const chaining
3	getSheetByName() DocumentApp Create (document)	for loop Variables – let and var
4	Logger.log	Arrays Getting specific values in arrays push
5	onOpen trigger getUi() createMenu() addItem() addToUi()	If else else if equals, and, or operators (===, &&, ||) ternery conditional

	activate() prompt() getSelectedButton() Button.OK getResponseText	length property
6	create() (sheet) openByUrl()	Global variables Scope for in loop
7	getName() toast() openById copy() (spreadsheet) rename() addEditor(), addEditors() addViewer(), addViewers() activate() (sheet) moveActiveSheet() getNumSheets() getSheets() deleteSheet()	---
8	getId() copyTo() hideColumns() hideRows() insertColumns() getLastRow() getMaxRows() deleteRows() getLastColumn() getMaxColumns()	shift()

	deleteColumns()	
	appendRow()	
	autoResizeColumn()	
	sort() (sheet)	
	ButtonSet.OK.CANCEL	
	getDataRange()	
	insertSheet()	
9	clearContent()	If() – present check
	newTrigger()	
	forSpreadsheet()	
	onFormSubmit()	
	create() (trigger)	
	setFormulaR1C1()	
	setNumberFormat()	
	setBorder()	
	onEdit trigger	
	e.range	
	getColumn()	
	getRow()	
	offset()	
	sort() (range)	
	setColumnWidth()	
	setWrap()	

This may not mean much to you at the moment, but it'll all become clearer as you start writing code.

Example files and full pieces of code

Links to all the files and full pieces of code used in this book can be found in Appendix 1.

The best way to learn is to start using it, so let's jump right in and write our first script.

CHAPTER 1 – First Script

Let's create our first script. Here, I want to show you how easy it is to write some code using Apps Script. This chapter is for those taking their first steps into writing code, so I will explain everything step-by-step.

First Google Apps Script

First, you'll need to open the **Script editor** where you'll be writing your code. This can be found in various places, but here we're going to be using a spreadsheet, so create a new Google Sheet, by clicking on the New button in Drive.

Then select Google Sheets.

- Folder
- File upload
- Folder upload

- Google Docs
- Google Sheets

Once opened, click on the "Tools" menu, and select the **Script editor**.

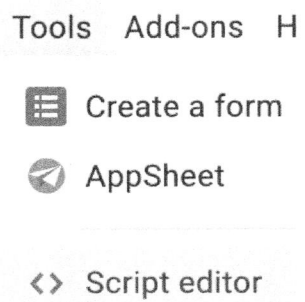

Open the **Script editor** and you'll be presented with a screen like this:

The main grey part of the page is where the script is written. By default, it already adds a bit of code in there for you. I'll explain the editor more in later chapters, but for now I'll show you how to write a short piece of code and get it running. Let's go through it step-by-step.

In the grey area, you have a little bit of code ready for you. We'll leave what's already on the page, as all programs need a **function** to run the code. A **function** is just a way of grouping a bunch of code together, then by giving it a name you'll be able to tell the computer what piece of code to run.

```
1    function myFunction() {
2
3    }
4
```

Lines 1-3: The syntax for this is, **function** plus the name of your function plus two parenthesis and then two curly brackets. Here the default function is called *myFunction* but you can name it almost whatever you like. In between the two curly brackets, is where you put your code. They show the start and end of this particular function.

What we're going to do in this little piece of code, is add the text *Hello* to cell A1 in the spreadsheet. To do this, we will need to:

- get the active spreadsheet
- get the active sheet
- get the range (cell)
- add the text to the cell

Note, the structure here, we're getting the overall spreadsheet, then getting a particular sheet within that spreadsheet. Then, we're telling it which particular range we want on that sheet, then finally stating what text we want to add.

This is the fundamental structure of working with spreadsheets.

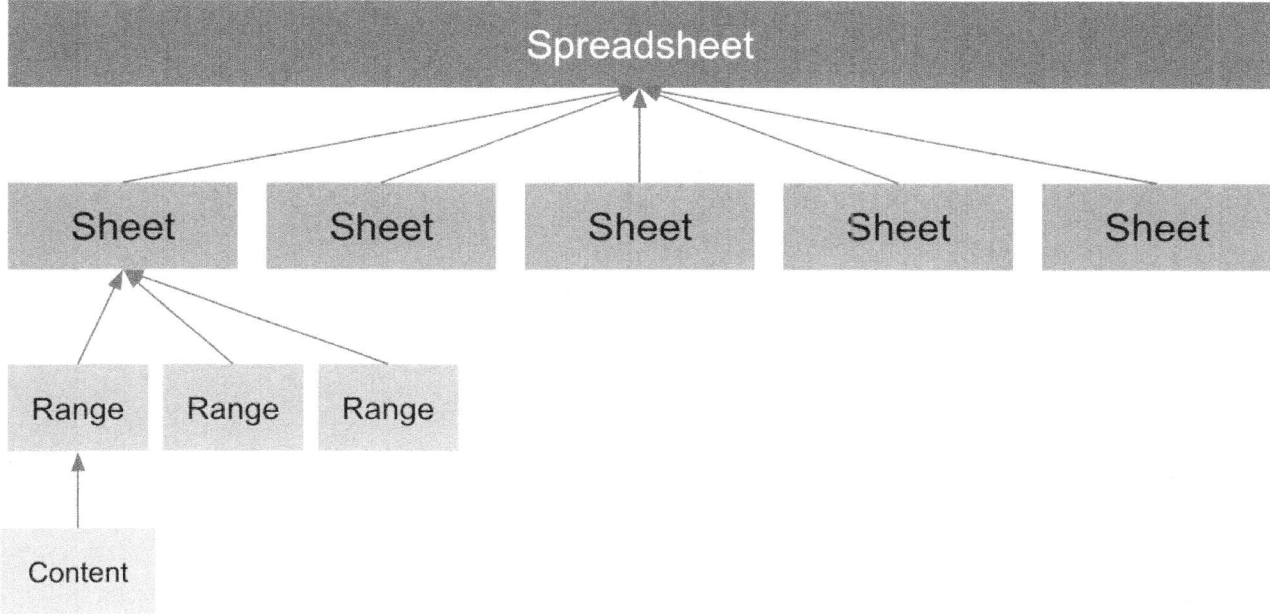

To do this, we're going to add just one line of code.

First, let's change the name of the function to *firstScript*. Double-click on the default name *myFunction* to select it.

```
function myFunction() {
```

Then type in the new name.

```
1    function firstScript() {
```

First, we need to state that we're going to be working with the a spreadsheet.

```
1  function firstScript() {
2      SpreadsheetApp
3  }
4
```

Line 2: Type in **SpreadsheetApp**. This is what is called a **Class** and is the top-level of the structure and the **SpreadsheetApp** tells the computer that we want to work with a spreadsheet. Make sure you use a capital S and a capital A with the rest being lowercase.

Then follow it with a dot. When you type the dot, the menu will change to show the options available to add to the spreadsheet. This is the **content assist**, which helps you write the code quicker by offering you the possible options and where you can click on them to save you typing them.

```
1  function firstScript() {
2      SpreadsheetApp.
3  }
4
```

We want to get the active spreadsheet, so start typing **getActiveSpreadsheet**.

As you can see as soon as you start typing the options are filtered by the letters you enter. We can see that there are a few **methods** that start with *getActive* and the one we want is **getActiveSpreadsheet**.

So, click on that to add it. You can just type the whole name. This will add it next to what you've already written.

Methods

Let's just take a moment to talk about **methods**. These are just specific instructions telling the computer what to do. **Methods** are a level below a **class** (e.g. SpreadsheetApp) and as you will see we can attach lots a methods to a class. What you will see in Apps Script is that the names of the **methods** are very intuitive and in most cases, are written in plain English and describe what they do.

The **methods** are written in **Camel Case**. What's that? The first word is in lowercase and the first letter of words after it have a capital letter. So, the method we just used was written like this **getActiveSpreadsheet**. This makes it easier to read and must be written like this as JavaScript and Apps Script are case-sensitive. Classes are written with the first letter capitalized (e.g. SpreadsheetApp).

Methods also need a pair of brackets attached to them at the end. Sometimes they will contain content, as we will see later, but this particular one is just empty. When you type the opening bracket, the editor will automatically add the closing pair, as these always go in pairs, and it's a common error to make, to forget to write the closing pair, this helps prevent that.

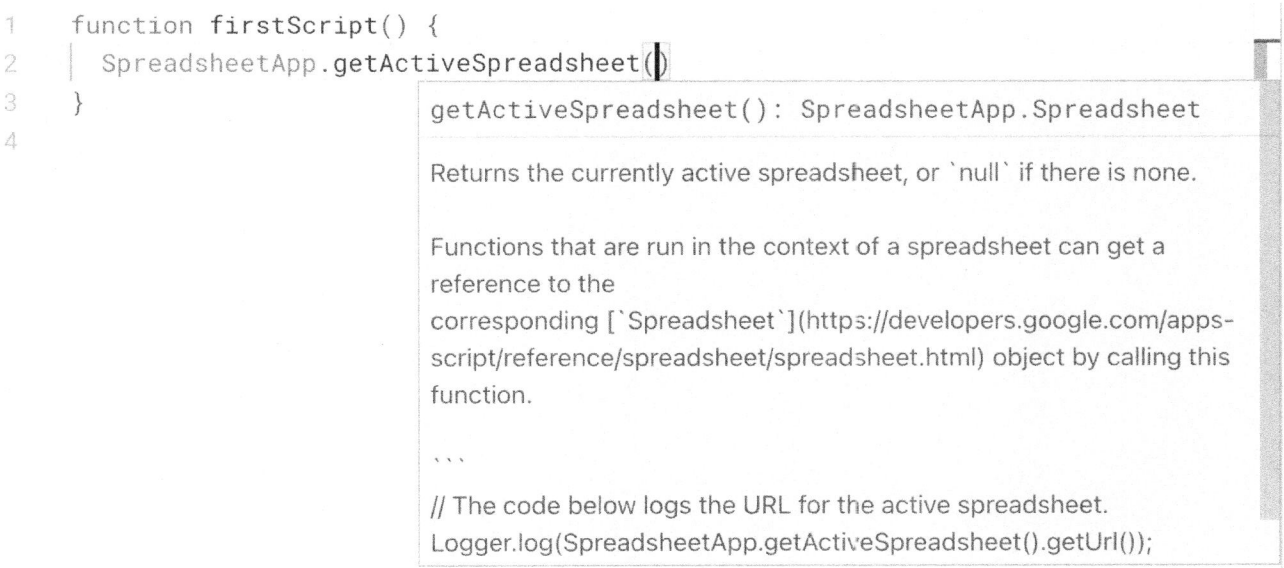

OK, back to our code.

You will also see that when we add the opening bracket, the dialogue box shows us some information about the method, and an example of code to show how it can be used.

OK, now we need to add the active sheet. Type a dot again and you will see the drop-down menu with options we can add to an active spreadsheet.

```
2    SpreadsheetApp.getActiveSpreadsheet().
3    }
4
```

Type in **getActiveSheet()**. As you see, we get information about this method.

```
1  function firstScript() {
2    SpreadsheetApp.getActiveSpreadsheet().getActiveSheet()
3  }
4
```

getActiveSheet(): SpreadsheetApp.Sheet

Gets the active sheet in a spreadsheet.

The active sheet in a spreadsheet is the sheet that is being displayed in the spreadsheet UI.

```
var sheet = SpreadsheetApp.getActiveSpreadsheet().getActiveSheet();
```

Next, we need to get the cell we want to add the text into. We do this by getting the range. Type a dot and then **getRange()**.

```
1    function firstScript() {
2        SpreadsheetApp.getActiveSpreadsheet().getActiveSheet().getRange()
3    }
4
```

> getRange(**row: any**, column: any):
> SpreadsheetApp.Range
>
> The row index of the cell to return; row indexing starts with 1.
>
> Returns the range with the top left cell at the given coordinates.
>
> ...
>
> var ss = SpreadsheetApp.getActiveSpreadsheet();
> var sheet = ss.getSheets()[0];
> // Passing only two arguments returns a "range" with a single cell.
> var range = sheet.getRange(1, 1);
> var values = range.getValues();
> Logger.log(values[0][0]);

There are different ways to get a range, but here we'll start with the simplest, which is to add the cell reference A1. To do that, we need to add it as text (a string), so first we add a quote mark. Like parenthesis, the editor will automatically add the second pair of quotes, as these have to be in pairs.

```
preadsheet().getActiveSheet().getRange("")
```

> getRange(**a1Notation: string**):
> SpreadsheetApp.Range

Then type in the cell reference in the middle of the quotes.

```
1    function firstScript() {
2        SpreadsheetApp.getActiveSpreadsheet().getActiveSheet().getRange("A1")
3    }
4
```

The final part is to add the Hello text to the cell. Type a dot.

```
sheet().getActiveSheet().getRange("A1").
```

> ◇ activate   (method)
> ◇ activateAsCurrentCell
> ◇ addDeveloperMetadata
> ◇ applyColumnBanding
> ◇ applyRowBanding
> ◇ autoFill

Then type in the method **setValue()**.

```
dsheet().getActiveSheet().getRange("A1").setValue()
```

setValue(**value: Object**): SpreadsheetApp.Range

The value for the range.

Sets the value of the range. The value can be numeric, string, boolean or date. If it begins
with `'='` it is interpreted as a formula.

In the brackets, type the text Hello in between quote marks, as it's text.

```
.setValue("Hello")
```

At the end of the line, we need to add a semi-colon. This basically shows that we are at the end of this particular set of instructions.

```
("Hello");
```

So, you should now have a one line which gets the active spreadsheet, the active sheet, the cell A1, and adds Hello in that cell.

```
1  function firstScript() {
2    SpreadsheetApp.getActiveSpreadsheet().getActiveSheet().getRange("A1").setValue("Hello");
3  }
4
```

Save the code by clicking on the disk icon in the toolbar. Ctrl + S (Mac: Cmd + S) will also save it.

Renaming a project

When we first open the script editor, the project is called "Untitled project" by default. Always rename it. Click on "Untitled project".

Then type in a new name for the project.

Rename Project

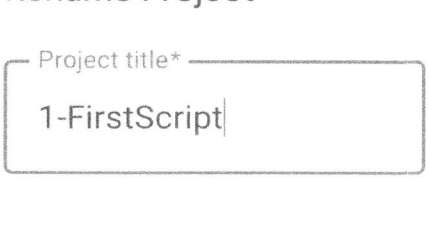

Cancel   Rename

Authorizing a script

Our script is almost ready to run, but first we need to authorize it. You need to do this the first time you run a script. Click on "Run" from the toolbar.

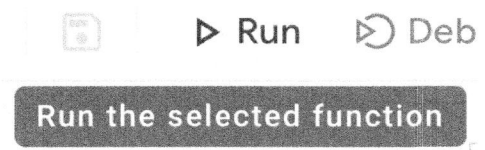

The Authorization required dialogue box will appear. Click on "Review permissions".

Authorization required

This project requires your permission to access your data.

Cancel Review permissions

This will ask which account to want to use. Usually the account you're currently in will appear. Just click on that.

Choose an account

to continue to 1-FirstScript

Barrie Roberts
bazrobertsbooks@gmail.com

Use another account

It will state that Google hasn't verified the app, which is normal and for most code you write, isn't necessary. Click on "Advanced".

Google hasn't verified this app

The app is requesting access to sensitive info in your Google Account. Until the developer (bazrobertsbooks@gmail.com) verifies this app with Google, you shouldn't use it.

Advanced   BACK TO SAFETY

Then click on the scary sounding "Go to 1-FirstScript (unsafe)". Don't worry it is safe, as it's your code!

Hide Advanced   BACK TO SAFETY

Continue only if you understand the risks and trust the developer (bazrobertsbooks@gmail.com).

Go to 1-FirstScript (unsafe)

This will confirm what the project will be allowed to do. So, in this simple example, it's asking you to give permission to see, edit, create and delete your spreadsheets in your Google Drive. Really we're only doing the first two things, but it's part of the same permissions.

Click "Allow".

1-FirstScript wants to access your Google Account

bazrobertsbooks@gmail.com

This will allow 1-FirstScript **to:**

- See, edit, create, and delete your spreadsheets in Google Drive ⓘ

Make sure you trust 1-FirstScript

You may be sharing sensitive info with this site or app. Learn about how 1-FirstScript will handle your data by reviewing its terms of service and privacy policies. You can always see or remove access in your Google Account.

Learn about the risks

Cancel   Allow

The program will then run and you will see the Execution log open below your code. For this code, it will just tell you when it started and finished. It will also show you if the program didn't complete due to any errors in the code. More on this later in the book.

Now open the spreadsheet, and we will see that we've add Hello to cell A1 programmatically.

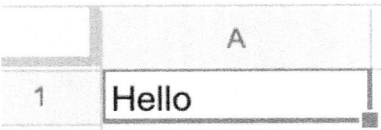

Well done! You've created your first script! Not the most exciting I know, but it has introduced you to not only how to write a script but also the basic structure of building up a piece of code.

CHAPTER 2 – Variables and getting & setting values

In this chapter, we're going look at how **variables** are set up and how they can store various pieces of information. We're also going to look at reading and writing data to and from a spreadsheet, which is one of the most common tasks when working with one.

I'm going to use a simple example, where we have some data about three different students and we want to put all that data together in one single table in a different part of a sheet. Then, we're going to format it a little bit to make it look better.

So, we will be getting data from these columns:

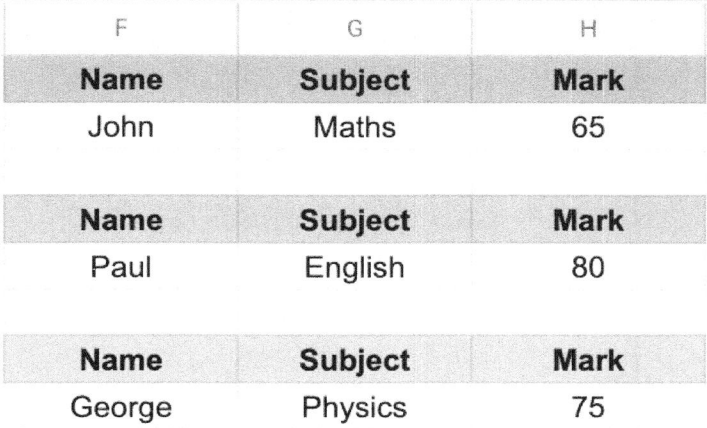

And writing it into these columns:

	A	B	C
1	**Name**	**Subject**	**Mark**
2	John	Maths	65
3	Paul	English	80
4	George	Physics	75

So first of all, what is a **variable**? It's basically a container that stores information. You give it a name and state what's in the container. There are three keywords to do this, **var**, **let**, and **const**. As a general rule, if the value of your **variable** isn't going to change, use the **const**, and this will help prevent errors, as **var** and **let** can be reassigned by accident.

All **variables** start with the keyword followed by the name for that **variable**. You can call your **variable** pretty much anything you like, except using keywords, like *function*, or starting it with a character that isn't a letter, for example a number. As we saw in the first chapter with the names of the methods, like **getActiveSheet(), variables** are usually written in camel case. You'll notice keywords in the script editor are shown in blue.

```
1  function settingConstants() {
2    const studentsName = "Paul";
3    const numberOfStudents = 4;
4  }
```

Above, we have two examples of **variables**. The first is a **variable** called *studentsName* and we have assigned the name *Paul* to that **variable**. So, every time we refer to *studentsName* we are referring to the name *Paul*. The same goes for numbers. The second **variable** is called *numberOfStudents* and we have stated that the number of students is 4.

Note, that text (or a "**string**") is written between quote marks. Note, single or double quote marks can be used. Numbers don't need quote marks, if they are being used as numbers. We use the *equals sign* to show that the text or the number has been assigned to that **variable**. In other words, that is what has been put in that particular container. The equals sign doesn't mean *equals to* as in maths. For that a double (==) or triple (===) equals sign is used. More about that in a later chapter.

The Code

Create a new spreadsheet and open the script editor from the Tools menu.

```
1. function collateMarks() {
2.   const ss = SpreadsheetApp.getActiveSpreadsheet();
3.
4. }
```

Line 1: Leave the default **function** text in there and change the **function** name from *myFunction* to *collateMarks*.

Line 2: In between the curly brackets, I've created a **variable** called *ss* and I've assigned the **SpreadsheetApp** class and the **getActiveSpreadsheet() method** to it.

So, why have I done that? **SpreadsheetApp.getActiveSpreadsheet()** refers to the current active spreadsheet, i.e. the one we're currently using. What a **variable** allows me to do is, instead of writing out **SpreadsheetApp.getActiveSpreadsheet()** every time I want to refer to it, I can put it in a **variable** and just refer to that **variable** from then on. So, every time I refer to *ss* from then on, I'm actually referring to the active spreadsheet.

It's common practice to see the **variable** *ss* used to refer to the spreadsheet. These common practices help you read and understand other people's code and for them to understand yours.

Next, as we're going to refer to the sheet numerous times when reading and writing data to and from it, let's store the active sheet in a **variable** called *sheet*. We now need to get the active sheet, so we need the **getActiveSheet()** method. We could write it out long hand like this:

SpreadsheetApp.getActiveSpreadsheet().getActiveSheet() but as we already have the first part stored in the **variable** *ss*, we can just use that.

```
1.  function collateMarks() {
2.    const ss = SpreadsheetApp.getActiveSpreadsheet();
3.    const sheet = ss.getActiveSheet();
4.  }
```

Line 3: Type in **const** and *sheet* followed by the equals sign. Then let's define this **variable**. Type *ss* followed by a dot. As we can see below it brings up the possible **methods** we can use with the spreadsheet.

```
ss.
    addDeveloperMetadata
    addEditor
    addEditors
  s addMenu
  s addViewer
```

Start typing the **method** we want, i.e. **getActiveSheet()** and when you see it in the menu click on it to add it.

```
ss.getA
         getActiveCell
         getActiveRange
         getActiveRangeList
         getActiveSheet
```

Then end the line with a semi-colon.

OK, now we want to start to create our table in a sheet. At the end of line 3, press enter a couple of times, so that you produce a couple of empty lines and which will move the curly bracket down a few lines.

Line 5: Type *sheet* followed by a dot.

```
sheet.
         activate
         addDeveloperMetadata
         appendRow
```

This refers to the current active sheet. We then need to get a range on that sheet.

```
1.  function collateMarks() {
2.    const ss = SpreadsheetApp.getActiveSpreadsheet();
3.    const sheet = ss.getActiveSheet();
4.
5.    sheet.getRange("A1").setValue("Name");
```

After the dot, type in **getRange()** and in the brackets add the cell reference "A1". Then type a dot, **setValue()** and in the brackets type "Name". Finally, end the line with a semi-colon.

This will get the cell *A1* and set its value to the word *Name*. In other words, it will write the word *Name* in cell A1 on our sheet, like this:

	A
1	Name

```
5.    sheet.getRange("A1").setValue("Name");
6.    sheet.getRange("B1").setValue("Subject");
7.    sheet.getRange("C1").setValue("Mark");
```

Lines 6 and 7 are similar. We get cells B1 and C1 and write the words *Subject* and *Mark*. It sets up the header row like this:

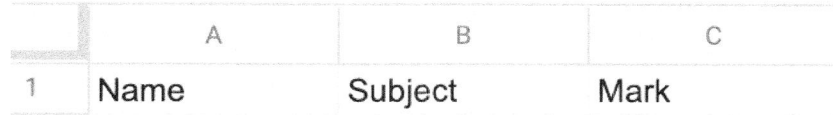

Now we have our header row, let's get the student data from columns F to H.

```
9.    const student1 = sheet.getRange("F2:H2").getValues();
```

Line 9: Here, I'm going to create another **variable** called *student1*. This time I'm going to get the data in a row of 3 cells (F2 to H2). As there is more than one piece of data, we use the **method** called **getValues()**. Note, the 's' on the end, it's a common mistake to forget to add the 's'.

This will store the three pieces of information: *John, Maths, 65* in the **variable** *student1*. Yes, **variables** can store more than one bit of information!

```
9.    const student1 = sheet.getRange("F2:H2").getValues();
10.   const student2 = sheet.getRange("F5:H5").getValues();
11.   const student3 = sheet.getRange("F8:H8").getValues();
```

Lines 10 to 11: We then do the same for the other two students. Now, we have the 3 details of the three students in three different **variables**, *student1*, *student2*, and *student3*.

Now, we've read the data in the sheet and stored it, we need to write it on the other part of the sheet.

```
13.   sheet.getRange("A2:C2").setValues(student1);
```

Line 13: I want to write the first student's data in row 2, so I get the range A2 to C2 and then set the values of those cells to the contents of the **variable** *student1*. So, what will happen is that in cell A2 *John* will be written, in B2 *Maths* and in C2 *65*, as we can see below:

	A	B	C
1	Name	Subject	Mark
2	John	Maths	65

```
13.   sheet.getRange("A2:C2").setValues(student1);
14.   sheet.getRange("A3:C3").setValues(student2);
15.   sheet.getRange("A4:C4").setValues(student3);
```

Lines 14-15: We carry out the same process for the other two students, this time writing the data to rows 3 and 4, by using the **variables** *student2* and *student3*. So, now we have our basic table:

	A	B	C
1	Name	Subject	Mark
2	John	Maths	65
3	Paul	English	80
4	George	Physics	75

That's how to get and set values on a sheet but let's make the table a little prettier by adding some formatting.

```
17.    const header = sheet.getRange("A1:C1");
```

Line 17: First, let's get the header row, which is A1 to C1. We use the **getRange()** method and store that range in the **variable** *header*. This means we don't have to get that range every time we use it, we can just refer to the **variable** *header*. Now, we have that header range we can use it to then add some formatting to it.

```
17.    header.setBackground("yellow")
18.          .setFontWeight("bold");
```

Line 18: Let's change the background colour to yellow. To do this, we get the header range (*header*) and use the **method setBackground()**. Then, we put the colour we want in the brackets with quote marks. Note, I've not added a semi-colon at the end. This is because I'm going to connect another **method** to it. This is called **chaining**.

Line 19: Let's also add bolding to the words. To do this, we use the **setFontWeight() method** and in the brackets we add the word *bold* in quote marks. This time we end it with a semi-colon.

As we can see, this has formatted the header.

	A	B	C
1	**Name**	**Subject**	**Mark**
2	John	Maths	65
3	Paul	English	80
4	George	Physics	75

Finally, let's align all the cells in the table centrally.

```
21.     const table = sheet.getRange("A1:C4");
```

Line 21: First, we need to get the range of cells in the table (A1 to C4). Here, I've stored that range in the **variable** *table*.

```
21.     const table = sheet.getRange("A1:C4");
22.     table.setHorizontalAlignment("center");
```

Line 22: We then get that table range, add the **setHorizontalAlignment()** method to it and in the brackets state *center* with quote marks.

So, let's run the program. This will read the data from one part of the sheet, write the data to another part, and finally format it all in one go. The first time we run it, it will ask us to authorize the access we want (see chapter 1 for details).

As we can see this has got the information on the 3 students, added a header, added the information on a different part of the sheet, added a yellow background and bolding to the header, and centered all our cells and the table looks much better.

	A	B	C
1	**Name**	**Subject**	**Mark**
2	John	Maths	65
3	Paul	English	80
4	George	Physics	75

By using **variables**, we were able to write a shorter piece of code and this code now also allows us to create a table with data for a different set of students.

Hopefully, you can see how easy it is to get data from a sheet and to write data to it.

When I was first learning JavaScript, I found the W3schools.com site extremely useful. It explains the language really well and every part has examples for you to try out. Bearing in mind, these are more focused towards using JavaScript with web pages, but the site taught me a lot very quickly.

If you want to learn more about **variables**, visit the W3schools site:

https://www.w3schools.com/js/js_const.asp

You can find the full piece of code for this chapter in Appendix 1.

CHAPTER 3 – Loops

In this chapter, we're going to look at loops and how they can make repetitive tasks really easy and how they can save you so much coding. One of the things computers are good at is doing repetitive tasks quickly and accurately.

For example, if we want to print the word *Hello!* a number of times down a column without a loop, we would have to repeat the same line of code for each of the rows, as you can see in the code below:

```
1.  function printHello() {
2.    const ss = SpreadsheetApp.getActiveSpreadsheet()
3.                                  .getSheetByName("Numbers");
4.    ss.getRange(1,1).setValue("Hello!");
5.    ss.getRange(2,1).setValue("Hello!");
6.    ss.getRange(3,1).setValue("Hello!");
7.    ss.getRange(4,1).setValue("Hello!");
8.    ss.getRange(5,1).setValue("Hello!");
9.    ss.getRange(6,1).setValue("Hello!");
10.   ss.getRange(7,1).setValue("Hello!");   //etc
11.
12. }
```

	A
1	Hello!
2	Hello!
3	Hello!
4	Hello!
5	Hello!
6	Hello!
7	Hello!
8	Hello!
9	Hello!
10	Hello!

The only thing changing each time is the row reference in the **getRange()** method. Imagine if we wanted to write this 100 times, that's a lot of code! With a loop, as we'll see in the examples below, we can simplify this to just 1 loop and 3 lines of code. A loop just allows you to repeat a section of code as many times as you like.

Below, we're going to look at seven simple examples of how loops can be used. In the spreadsheet linked to this chapter, there are 2 sheets, one called *Numbers* and the other called *Names*.

Loop 1 – Print "Hello!" 20 times down column A

```
1.  //Print Hello!" 20 times down column A
2.  function loop1() {
3.    const ss = SpreadsheetApp.getActiveSpreadsheet().getSheetByName("Numbers");
```

Open the script editor in your Google Sheet and replace the default code with the above one.

Line 1: We can write comments in our code to help us remember what it does. To make the computer ignore them, we use two back slashes **//** at the start. In the script editor, you'll see the text is in grey, to show it's a comment and will be ignore when the program is run.

Line 2: We start with the function and here let's call it *loop1*.

Line 3: Now, we want to get the sheet called *Numbers*. So, we use the **SpreadsheetApp** class, then get the active spreadsheet, then get the particular sheet we want, in this case called "Numbers". For that we use the **getSheetByName()** method and add the name between quotes in the brackets. I've stored it in the variable *ss*, as we're going to refer to the sheet again in the next part, so instead of writing out the SpreadsheetApp… part again, we can just use the variable name *ss*.

Now we want to set up a loop, which will add the word Hello! to cell A1, cell A2, and so on, down to cell A20. Here, we're going to use the common **for loop**.

There are two main parts: the counter, in this case counting from 1 to 20, and what you want the loop to do each time it goes around.

for (counter) {

  Stuff you want to happen every time around the loop

}

```
5.    for (r=1; r<21; r++) {
6.      ss.getRange(r,1).setValue("Hello!");
7.    }
8.  }
```

Line 5: Start with the keyword **for** then open the brackets. There are 3 parts within the brackets:

34

1. Starting point of the loop.
2. Condition you want to check; if it's true it continues the loop, if it's false it stops the loop and continues on with the program.
3. How much you want to increase the counter by, each time it goes around the loop.

The counter needs something to keep count, so we use a variable to do that. A variable like a variable is a pot to store something, like a number, but the key difference is that it can change, whereas, a variable cannot.

So, here we have the variable *r* (for rows) and we're starting at 1, as we want to start at row 1.

Then, we want to continue until 20, so the condition will be to continue while the variable *r* is less than 21.

As we want to put the name in all the rows, we want to increase *r* by 1 each time, so that it will print *Hello!* on row 1, row 2, row 3, etc. Here, I've used the common shorthand way to increase a value by 1, i.e. using a double + after the variable (r++). This is the same as saying *r+=1*.

All of this is contained in parenthesis and this is what controls the counting within the loop.

Then, we need to tell it what to do, during each loop. To do this, we use the curly brackets, so we open the curly bracket ready to put some instructions in it.

```
5.    for (r=1; r<21; r++) {
6.      ss.getRange(r,1).setValue("Hello!");
7.    }
8. }
```

Line 6: Now, we want to get the range and set its value to the word *Hello!*. So, first we get the sheet we want using the variable ss, then use the **getRange()** method. Here, we're going to use the **getRange()** method, that needs a row and column, to determine which cell it is.

In the brackets, we have two arguments: (*row number, column number*). The column will always be the same, so we write 1, for the first column, A. But the row we want to change each time we go around the loop, so we use the variable *r* from our **for loop**. Then we set the value of that cell with the word *Hello!*.

Line 7: We close the **for loop** with a closed curly bracket.

35

Line 8: We close the function in the same way, with a closed curly bracket. So, you can see that the function does everything within its curly brackets, and the **for loop** does everything within its curly brackets.

When we run the code, the first time around the loop, *r* will be 1, so the range it will get will be row 1, column 1 (i.e. cell A1). Then, it will add *Hello!* in that cell. The counter *r* will go up by one, then the second time it goes around the loop *r* will be 2, so it will get row 2, column 1 (i.e. cell A2), and so on, until it reaches row 20. Then the condition will be false, as r will be 21 and isn't less than 21, so it will continue down the program.

Let's run the code and see what happens. As I've already set up the 7 different loops in this project, I need to select the function *loop1* to run it. If you're using the my file, you may need to select the *loop1* function.

So, from the toolbar to the right of where it says debug, if it doesn't say loop1, "click on the menu to select the *loop1* function.

Then click the Run button to run the code.

The first time you run it you'll have to authorize the script as explained in chapter 1.

	A
1	Hello!
2	Hello!
3	Hello!
4	Hello!
5	Hello!
6	Hello!
7	Hello!
8	Hello!
9	Hello!
10	Hello!
11	Hello!
12	Hello!
13	Hello!
14	Hello!
15	Hello!
16	Hello!
17	Hello!
18	Hello!
19	Hello!
20	Hello!

As we can see it's written Hello! in cells A1 to A20, just as we wanted.

Loop 2 – Print numbers 1 to 20 down column A

This time let's use the numbers in the loop and add them to the sheet, i.e. write numbers 1 to 20 in the cells in column A.

```
10.   //Print numbers 1 to 20 down column A
11.   function loop2() {
12.     const ss =
      SpreadsheetApp.getActiveSpreadsheet().getSheetByName("Numbers");
```

Lines 11 to 14: Same as loop 1, except call it loop 2.

```
14.     for (r=1; r<21; r++) {
15.       ss.getRange(r,1).setValue(r);
16.     }
17.   }
```

Line 15: This time, we want to set the value of the cells to be the current number in the loop. So, we get the range as before, and this time set the value to be the variable *r*. So, the first time around the loop, *r* will be 1, so it will put 1 in row 1. the second time it will be 2, so it will be 2, etc.

Lines 16-17: We close the loop and function as before.

Select loop2 from the toolbar and run the program.

	A
1	1
2	2
3	3
4	4
5	5
6	6
7	7
8	8
9	9
10	10
11	11
12	12
13	13
14	14
15	15
16	16
17	17
18	18
19	19
20	20

As we can see it added the numbers 1 to 20 to column A.

Loop 3 – Fill cells A1 to A20 in blue

It's not just values that we can use loops with. Let's add some colour to our sheet.

```
19.   //Fill cells A1 to A20 in blue
20.   function loop3() {
21.     const ss =
    SpreadsheetApp.getActiveSpreadsheet().getSheetByName("Numbers");
```

Lines 20-21: As before.

```
23.     for (r=1; r<21; r++) {
24.       ss.getRange(r,1).setBackground("blue");
25.     }
26.   }
```

Line 23: As before.

Line 24: This gets the range as before, but this time set the background colour to blue, using the **setBackground()** method.

Select loop3 from the toolbar and run the program. As we can see it's filled the cells in blue.

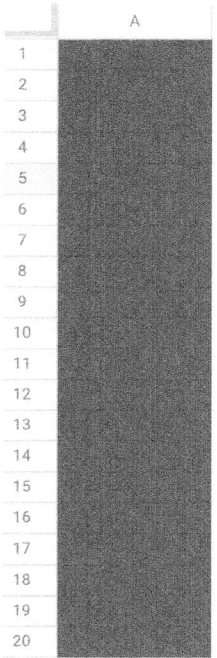

Loop 4 – Fill cells A1 to A20 in blue and print numbers 1 to 20

We can carry out more than one instruction within our loop. Let's fill the cells with blue and add the numbers 1 to 20.

```
28.   //Fill cells A1 to A20 in blue and print numbers 1 to 20
29.   function loop4() {
30.     const ss =
      SpreadsheetApp.getActiveSpreadsheet().getSheetByName("Numbers");
```

Lines 29-30: As before.

```
32.     for (r=1; r<21; r++) {
33.       ss.getRange(r,1).setBackground("blue")
34.                       .setValue(r);
35.     }
36.   }
```

Line 32: As before.

Line 33: Similar to loop3, we set the background colour, but this time, don't add a semi-colon at the end of the line. This allows us to add other instructions to the same range.

Line 34: Type dot and the method you want, in this case, **setValue()**. Here, we're going to add the variable *r*, i.e. the current number in the loop, to the cell. This time, add a semi-colon at the end.

Note, the **setBackground()** and **setValue()** methods are both linked to the **getRange()** method, as we didn't use a semi-colon after the **setBackground()** one.

Select loop4 from the toolbar and run the program. As we can see, it added both the colour and the numbers.

Loop 5 – Print the numbers 1 to 20 across 10 different columns

So far, we've just added values and colours down the same column but we can of course move across the columns too. Here, we're going to look at how two **for loops** can be used together, to add numbers down the columns and to add them to different columns across the page.

```
38.     //Print 10 columns of numbers 1 to 20
39.     function loop5() {
40.       const ss =
        SpreadsheetApp.getActiveSpreadsheet().getSheetByName("Numbers");
```

Lines 39-40: As above.

```
42.       for (c=1; c<11; c++) {
43.
44.         for (r=1; r<21; r++) {
45.           ss.getRange(r,c).setValue(r);
46.         }
47.       }
48.     }
```

Lines 44-46: This is pretty much the same loop from loop2, i.e. it will add numbers from 1 to 20 down a column. The only exception is that instead of keeping the column value as a variable 1, I've added the variable c (for column), which will change as the loop goes around.

Lines 42 and 47: Wrapped around the above loop, we have another loop which will change the column number from 1 to 10, or in other words from column A to J. Here, I've called the variable c and it starts at column 1, then increase by 1 until it reaches the tenth column (i.e. c less than 11).

Running the loop5 script, we can see that it added the numbers 1 to 20 to column A, then to column B, and so on until column J (the tenth column).

	A	B	C	D	E	F	G	H	I	J
1	1	1	1	1	1	1	1	1	1	1
2	2	2	2	2	2	2	2	2	2	2
3	3	3	3	3	3	3	3	3	3	3
4	4	4	4	4	4	4	4	4	4	4
5	5	5	5	5	5	5	5	5	5	5
6	6	6	6	6	6	6	6	6	6	6
7	7	7	7	7	7	7	7	7	7	7
8	8	8	8	8	8	8	8	8	8	8
9	9	9	9	9	9	9	9	9	9	9
10	10	10	10	10	10	10	10	10	10	10
11	11	11	11	11	11	11	11	11	11	11
12	12	12	12	12	12	12	12	12	12	12
13	13	13	13	13	13	13	13	13	13	13
14	14	14	14	14	14	14	14	14	14	14
15	15	15	15	15	15	15	15	15	15	15
16	16	16	16	16	16	16	16	16	16	16
17	17	17	17	17	17	17	17	17	17	17
18	18	18	18	18	18	18	18	18	18	18
19	19	19	19	19	19	19	19	19	19	19
20	20	20	20	20	20	20	20	20	20	20

So, how does this work exactly?

```
42.     for (c=1; c<11; c++) {
43.
44.       for (r=1; r<21; r++) {
45.         ss.getRange(r,c).setValue(r);
46.       }
47.     }
48.   }
```

At the start, *c* is 1 and *r* is 1, so it gets the cell A1, and adds the number 1 (*r*) in the cell. It then gets trapped in the *r* loop, and goes around that one a second time. So, this time *c* is still 1, but *r* is now 2, so it adds 2 (*r*) to cell A2. It continues around the *r* loop until it hits 20, then it goes down a line and hits the end curly bracket of the *c* loop (line 47).

It then goes back to line 42 and goes around again. This time *c* is now 2, and the *r* loop is reset back to 1. It goes around the *r* loop like before until it hits 20, then it goes back to the *c* loop, which will now be 3, and so on, until the *c* loop hits 10. At which point it finishes.

Loops within loops can be complicated to follow and if I'm struggling to follow what's happening, I usually look at it step by step and see what's happening to the variables each time they go around the loop.

Loop 6 – Create 5 documents and name them Document1 to Document5

Now we've covered the real basics, let's see what else you can do with a loop. Adding numbers and colours to a sheet is fine, but you can do so much more with them. Here, let's create some Google Docs and number them individually from our loop.

```
50.    //Create 5 documents naming them Document1 to Document5
51.    function loop6() {
52.      const ss =
         SpreadsheetApp.getActiveSpreadsheet().getSheetByName("Numbers");
```

Lines 51-52: As above.

```
54.      for (r=1; r<6; r++) {
55.        DocumentApp.create("Document"+r);
56.      }
57.    }
```

Line 54: I want to create 5 documents, so let's set the condition to less than 6.

Line 55: Every time it loops, we want it to create a document and name it "Document" plus the current number from the variable *r*, i.e. Document1, Document2, etc. To create a new Google Doc we use the **DocumentApp** class and the **create()** method. In the brackets, we state the name we want to give the document. So, it will be "Document" plus the number from *r*.

Lines 56-57: We close the loop and function as before.

Running the loop6 script, we will see in our My Drive, 5 new documents, all titled individually, 1 to 5.

- Document1
- Document2
- Document3
- Document4
- Document5

Loop 7 – Create 4 documents each with names from the sheet

It's not just numbers we can add to our documents, but we can also get text from our sheet and name the documents accordingly. Here, we're going to create documents for 4 students and append each document title with their name.

```
59.  //Create 4 documents each with student's name (use sheet called Names)
60.  function loop7() {
61.    const ss = SpreadsheetApp.getActiveSpreadsheet().getSheetByName("Names");
```

Line 61: Use the *Names* sheet for this one, where I've already added the names of the 4 students.

	A
1	Joan
2	Paula
3	Dingo
4	Georgina

```
63.    for (r=1; r<5; r++) {
64.      let studentName = ss.getRange(r,1).getValue();
65.      DocumentApp.create("Document-"+studentName);
66.    }
67.  }
```

Line 63: Set the **for loop** up to count from 1 to 4.

Line 64: First, we need to get the student's name from the sheet. We'll get a different name every time we go around the loop. Set up a variable called *studentName*. Instead of using the keyword **const**, like we've been using, we use the keyword **let**, as this will change as it goes round the loop.

Note, you will see a lot of code on the internet that uses the keyword **var** (for variable). Originally, to set variables, you could only use **var**, but in the latest version of JavaScript, **let**, **const**, and **var** can be used. I'll explain this a little more at the end of the chapter, but for now, **var** works in a very similar way to **let** and as a beginner, you could use either. I will use **let** in this book as it's the more correct one to use for this situation.

Back to Line 64: Get the range which is *r*, 1. So, the first time around the loop it will get the name in row 1, column 1, i.e. "Joan", the second time it will get row 2, column 1, i.e. "Paula", and so on. then get the value in that cell, i.e. the name.

Line 65: Then using **DocumentApp.create()** we create a new document, which will be titled "Document-" plus the student's name.

Line 66-67: As always, we close the loop and function.

Run the loop7 script. As we can see, in our My Drive, it's created 4 documents individually titled for each of our students.

- Document-Dingo
- Document-Georgina
- Document-Joan
- Document-Paula

The important thing here is that we are getting information from a sheet, using a loop to move around the sheet to get different bits of information and then using it elsewhere. This is extremely useful and allows you to do all sorts of things.

To summarize the use of **const**, **let**, and **var**:

const – This is used to store data values that do not change during the script. If you try to change it or try to assign it again with a different value, it will throw an error. There are exceptions to this, but we'll see that in a later chapter. This prevents possible reassigning errors in your code.

let – This is used to store values that might or will change in the script.

var – This is also used to store values that might or will change in the script.

Scope

The main difference between **let** and **var** is **scope**. What's that? There are different levels within a piece of code, and for example, variables assigned in a function, as we've been doing so far, can only be seen in that function and not in other functions or outside it. The same is true for other {} blocks, like loops.

If a variable is assigned inside one, it has a different scope to if it was assigned outside it, kind of like a different level. Variables declared in a {} block can be "seen" outside the {} block when **var** is used, but not when **let** is used.

For example, let's look at a simple loop which declares two variables in it, v and l, using **var** and using **let**. They get the current value of r and add either 1 or 2 to it. Then we will log the value of v and l after the loop has finished and importantly OUTSIDE the loop. (More about the **log** in the next chapter).

```
14.    for (r=1; r<21; r++) {
15.      ss.getRange(r,1).setValue(r);
16.      var v = r+1;
17.      let l = r+1;
18.    }
19.    Logger.log(v);
20.    Logger.log(l);
```

Run the function and you will see in the execution log two things:

```
21.0
```

```
ReferenceError: l is not defined
varLetDifference   @   Code.gs:79
```

First, the **var** variable, v, was visible and it has logged the correct number, 21.

But the **let** variable, l, isn't visible, and so it has logged an error saying it isn't defined.

So, if we accidentally used **var** variable we could but potentially that could cause a problem if it's not the value we intended, whereas, we couldn't do that with the let one, this potentially preventing a problem.

Like **const**, the use of **let** can help reduce possible reassignment errors or accidentally using an incorrect value of a variable. For simple programs, it's not that important, but it's a good practice to get into early on.

If you want to learn more about **var** and **let** and **scope**, check out these pages on the W3schools site:

https://www.w3schools.com/js/js_variables.asp

https://www.w3schools.com/js/js_let.asp

If you want to learn more about **for loops** visit the W3schools site:

https://www.w3schools.com/js/js_loop_for.asp

You can find the full piece of code for this chapter in Appendix 1.

CHAPTER 4 – Arrays, Log & Executions

In this chapter, we're going to look at another key area in JavaScript and Apps Script and indeed in many coding languages, that of arrays, which are just special variables which allow you to store multiple elements in a single variable. I'll also introduce you to the Execution log, where you can see what's happening in your code without for example, having to print it on a sheet. Plus, see how long a script took in the Execution log and then see how we can speed up our scripts.

Introducing the Execution log

Following on from the last chapter on loops, let's take a look at some looped data in the log. Here we have some data in a sheet. We're going to loop down the data and put it one by one into the log.

	A
1	2
2	4
3	6
4	8
5	10
6	12
7	14
8	16
9	18
10	20
11	22
12	24
13	26
14	28
15	30
16	32
17	34
18	36
19	38
20	40

```
1. //Gets the numbers from the sheet and logs them in the log
2. function logNumbers(){
3.   const ss = SpreadsheetApp.getActiveSpreadsheet().getActiveSheet();
```

With all the examples in this chapter, we're going to get the active sheet, so line 3, you'll see repeated for each of the functions below. You'll use this line repeatedly for a lot of programs you write, where you're working with a spreadsheet and the current sheet.

```
5.      for (r=1; r<21; r++) {
6.          let numberFromSheet = ss.getRange(r,1).getValue();
```

Now, we want to loop down the list on the sheet.

Line 5: Here, we know we have 20 numbers, so we set the loop to start at row 1 and finish at row 20 (<21). Here, I've used the variable *r* as the counter.

Line 6: Then, we get the cell at that point in the loop using **getRange()** and a row and a column number. The row will be the variable *r* and the column will always be 1 as it's the first column, A. Then, we get its value and store it in the variable *numberFromSheet*.

```
8.          Logger.log(numberFromSheet);
9.      }
10. }
```

Line 8: Now, still within the loop we log the numbers in the log. This is easy to do, just use **Logger.log()** and in the brackets state what you want to add to it. In this case, it'll be the contents of the variable *numberFromSheet*.

Lines 9 and 10: We close the loop with the curly bracket and then the function with another one.

logNumbers ▼

  logNumbers
  array1a
  array1b
  array2
  array3
  array4a
  array4b

If you're using a copy of this file I'm using, you may need to select the function you want to run. If necessary click on the function drop-down menu from the toolbar and click "*logNumbers*". Then, click the Run button to run the function.

Underneath your code, you will see the Execution log appear.

Execution log

9:09:00 AM	Notice	Execution started
9:09:00 AM	Info	2.0
9:09:00 AM	Info	4.0
9:09:00 AM	Info	6.0
9:09:00 AM	Info	8.0
9:09:00 AM	Info	38.0
9:09:00 AM	Info	40.0
9:09:01 AM	Notice	Execution completed

As we can, it's logged the values each time in went around the loop. So, it got "2" from row 1, then "4" from row 2, and so on. Each time placing them in the log.

The log is an excellent way to debug your code and to see what's happening in your code and any point in it. You can put **Logger.log()** on any line and it's really useful to see what's going on, especially with what's being stored in your variables.

Single items and multiple items

OK, now we have a place where we can see our data, let's move on to look at arrays. In this example, we're going to look at storing individual and multiple items in variables. Note, we could use variables too.

```
12.   //Show a variable with 1 item and a variable with an array of items
13.   function array1a(){
14.     const ss = SpreadsheetApp.getActiveSpreadsheet().getActiveSheet();
15.   
16.     const item = "Fred";
17.     const items = ["Joan", "Paula", "Dingo", "Georgina"];
```

Lines 13-14: As above.

50

Line 16: Here, I've stored the text string "Fred" in the variable *item*.

Line 17: This time, I want to store 4 different names in the variable *items*. To do this, I need to set up an array. The contents of an array are shown by whatever is in between the square brackets. So, here we have four names all within one array called *items*. To separate them, you need to use commas and as these are words (strings) we'll need to use quote marks.

```
19.     Logger.log(item);
20.     Logger.log(items);
21. }
```

Lines 19-21: Now, let's log the two variables in the log and then close the function.

array1a ▼

Choose "array1a" from the toolbar and click Run.

Execution log

```
9:21:09 AM    Notice     Execution started

9:21:09 AM    Info       Fred

9:21:09 AM    Info       [Joan, Paula, Dingo, Georgina]

9:21:10 AM    Notice     Execution completed
```

As we can see, it shows the text string "Fred" and then the array below it. In the log, it displays the array with square brackets, so you know it's an array.

Accessing values in arrays

We often want to get at the information stored in an array. Let's see how we do that. Here, we're going to access the two variables *item* and *items* and add them to our sheet.

```
23. //Showing the difference between setting a single value and an array
24. function array1b(){
25.     const ss = SpreadsheetApp.getActiveSpreadsheet().getActiveSheet();
26.
```

```
27.     const item = "Fred";
28.     const items = ["Joan", "Paula", "Dingo", "Georgina"];
```

Lines 24-28: The same code as the previous example, except I've called this function *array1b*.

```
30.     ss.getRange("D1").setValue(item);
```

Line 30: Let's add the content of *item* to the cell D1.

```
32.     ss.getRange("E1").setValue(items);
```

Line 32: Now, let's do the same with the content of *items* to cell E1.

```
34.     ss.getRange("F1").setValue(items[1]);
35. }
```

Finally, let's get a specific item from our array and put it in cell F1. To do so, we need to state in which position in our array is the name we want. In arrays, each item of data has a position, starting in position **0**. So, "Joan" is at position 0, "Paula" is in position 1, and so on. A common mistake is to forget that arrays are zero-based, i.e. they start at 0 not at 1.

Line 34-35: So, for example, to get "Paula" we need to get the array items at position 1. We do that by stating the variable name and in square brackets stating its position, e.g. [1].

Run the code and let's see what we get.

D	E	F
Fred	Joan	Paula

"Fred" has been added in cell D1 as expected.

However, in cell E1 we were expecting to add the contents of *items* but we only have the first name in the array! This is because we're using **setValue()** which is expecting a single item. As we'll see below there are of course ways to access multiple data.

Finally, in cell F1 we wanted to add the second name on the list and we have indeed, so the index we used has worked.

Using getValues() and setValues() to get a range of values in one go

Here, we're going to get a range of values, add them to the log to see what they look like. Then, add those values to our sheet and pick out a value from that range and add it to the sheet.

```
37.    //Uses getValues to get an array of numbers in one go; How to add them to a
       sheet
38.    function array2(){
39.      const ss = SpreadsheetApp.getActiveSpreadsheet().getActiveSheet();
40.
41.      const listOfNumbers = ss.getRange(1,1,20).getValues();
```

Line 41: Let's get the range of numbers we had in the first example from column A.

Here, I'm using **getRange()** and stating the range in which those numbers are. The numbers in the brackets refer to: start row number, start column number, number of rows. So, it's row 1, column A (first column, and 20 rows. As we are only getting one column, we don't need to state the number of columns.

Then, as there is more than one value, we use **getValues()** to get all the values in one go and store them in *listOfNumbers*.

```
43.      Logger.log(listOfNumbers);
```

Line 43: Then, log the contents of *listOfNumbers*.

```
45.      ss.getRange(1,8,20).setValues(listOfNumbers);
```

Line 45: Now, let's add that range of numbers to our sheet. Here, I'm going to put them in column H (8th column). I get the range of cells I want to add to. Note, this has to be the same number of cells as the original data, otherwise, it will throw an error. Then, similar to **getValues()** we're going to use its opposite, **setValues()** to add the values to those cells.

```
47.      ss.getRange(1,9).setValue(listOfNumbers[1]);
48.    }
```

Line 47-48: Finally, let's extract a number from *listOfNumbers* and add it to cell I1. Similar to above, we'll need to use **setValue()** then state the variable name we want and the position in the data we want. So, here I want to get the second item, so I need to state position 1. Then close the function.

Run the code and you'll see the list of numbers has been added to column H and that we have picked the second number out and added it to cell I1.

In the log and we'll see that line 43 logged our data.

```
Info    [[2.0], [4.0], [6.0], [8.0], [10.0], [12.0], [14.0], [16.0], [18.0], [20.0],
        [22.0], [24.0], [26.0], [28.0], [30.0], [32.0], [34.0], [36.0], [38.0], [40.0]]
```

Note, that this time every number has a set of square brackets around it and that all the data is enclosed within a second set of brackets. This shows that the data is stored in lots of little arrays within 1 larger array, what is known as an **array of arrays**. This is why, we can use **setValues()** as here we have multiple items and we can add them to our sheet in one go. Whereas, in line 32 we couldn't use **setValues()** as the data was one item.

One way to think of this in relation to a spreadsheet is in terms of rows and columns. In a single array, the square brackets is one row, and the items in the array are different columns. In the example above, every pair of square brackets is a row, wrapped up in one pair of square brackets, to make it one array. This makes sense as the original data was indeed on different rows, with every number on a different one.

How arrays relate to rows and columns on a spreadsheet

Let's look how an array is related to a spreadsheet more closely. In this example, we're going to add one row of data, and then add two rows of data. The important thing is to notice the format of the arrays to do this and what it produces on the sheet.

```
50.   //Showing how arrays relate to rows and columns
51.   function array3(){
52.     const ss = SpreadsheetApp.getActiveSpreadsheet().getActiveSheet();
53.     const oneRowOfItems = [["Joan", "Paula", "Dingo", "Georgina"]];
54.     const twoRowsOfItems = [["Wilma", "Fred", "Betty", "Barney"], [35, 45, 30, 40]];
55.     ss.getRange(3,4,1,4).setValues(oneRowOfItems);
56.     ss.getRange(5,4,2,4).setValues(twoRowsOfItems);
57.   }
```

Lines 50-52: We get our sheet as before.

Line 53: This first array contains four names and they are stored in one array. That one array will be one row on the sheet. To be able to add that to the sheet, we need to wrap it up in another set of square brackets, so it's all one element for **setValues()** to recognize and use.

Line 54: This time we have two sets of data, one group of data with their names, and another with their ages. The two sets of data will be on two separate rows. In the array we show this by grouping the names in one array, adding a comma, then adding a second array. Then we wrap it all up in a pair of square brackets, so it becomes one array. This is what we saw in example array2, with the rows of data.

Line 55: To add it to the sheet, we need to get the range. Here, I'm going to add it D3:D7, which is row 3, column 4, there's only 1 row, and there are 4 items (or columns). Then we use **setValues()** to add the array contents.

Line 56: Similarly, we do the same for the second array, but this time add it to row 5. Plus, there are 2 arrays so there will be 2 rows, so change the third number in the getRange brackets to 2. The structure is exactly the same, despite this being an array of arrays.

Run the code and you will see the first row of data, and then underneath, the two rows of data.

Joan	Paula	Dingo	Georgina
Wilma	Fred	Betty	Barney
35	45	30	40

This is an important concept to understand, as it's key to adding and getting multiple data to and from a sheet.

Also, remember that **setValues()** expects the data to be wrapped up in two sets of square brackets, i.e. to be an array of arrays, even if it's just one row of data.

Looping through an array

A useful technique is to loop through an array, as we may want to get the individual elements, or even change the format of the array. In this example, we're going to loop through an array of names and add those names one by one to a sheet, with each name on a different row.

```
59.  //How to loop through an array
60.  function array4(){
61.    const ss = SpreadsheetApp.getActiveSpreadsheet().getActiveSheet();
62.    const items = ["Joan", "Paula", "Dingo", "Georgina"];
```

Lines 60-62: The same as *array1a*, we set up an array with 4 names.

```
64.    for (i=1; i<5; i++) {
65.      ss.getRange(i,11).setValue(items[i-1]);
66.    }
67.  }
```

Line 64: First, we set up a **for loop**. This will go from 1 to 4. Here, we're using the variable *i* to keep count. Note, that *i* is often used in loops, so you'll see it a lot when you look at code examples.

Line 65: Now, we want to get a cell on the sheet (we're going to use column K (11th column)) and set its value to one of the names in the array. So, first we get the range and get the cell location (11,1 > 11,2 > etc).

Then, we will set the value by getting the array items and getting one word at a time, starting at 0 (as arrays are zero-based, whereas rows and columns aren't), so we need to subtract 1 to get the array position, e.g. [0], [1], etc.

Lines 66-67: We close the loop and the function.

K
Joan
Paula
Dingo
Georgina

Run the code and as we can see, on the sheet, it has taken the contents of the array and added the names in each of the cells. This also shows us how we can change the format of the original data, as the four names were in one row, but we've changed it so it's one name across four rows.

Setting up an empty array and adding to it

Here, we're going to loop down one list, add the values one by one to an array, then add those values one by one to another part of the sheet. This will show you how we create empty arrays, and how we can add items to an array.

```
69.  //Getting values one by one from a sheet and one by one adding them to a
     sheet
70.  function array5a(){
71.    const ss = SpreadsheetApp.getActiveSpreadsheet().getActiveSheet();
72.    let listOfNames = [];
```

Line 72: First, let's set up an empty array. We do that, simply by assigning a pair of square brackets to it. So, at the moment the variable *listOfNames* is empty but it's an array. Note, I've used **let** to show that this isn't variable and will change as we add data to it.

```
74.    for (r=1; r<5; r++) {
```

Line 74: Then, let's set up our **for loop**, to count from 1 to 4.

```
76.      let name = ss.getRange(r,11).getValue();
77.      listOfNames.push(name);
```

During each loop, we will get the value from the cell on the sheet then add it to the array.

Line 76: First, we get the cell using the **getRange()** method using the row and column. As we want to go down the rows from 1 to 4, we add the variable *r* in the row part. The column will remain fixed as there is only one column (K the 11th column). Then we get its value. Make sure there is data in this column on your sheet.

Line 77: Now, we need to add it to the array. To do this, we use the array method **push()**. So, we state the name of the array we want to add to, then add a dot then the word *push*. In the brackets, we state what we want to add to the array. In this case, it will be the value we just got, which is in the variable *name*.

```
79.       Logger.log(listOfNames);
```

Line 79: I'm going to log the list of names as it's going around the loop, so we can see what's happening in the array.

```
81.       ss.getRange("M"+r).setValue(listOfNames[r-1]);
82.     }
83.   }
```

Line 81: Now, we get the cell we want on the sheet, this time in column M and the current row number r, and add the latest name in the array.

Note, we would normally just add the variable *name* here, but as we'll see in the next example, we can use the array to add the names in one go.

M
Joan
Paula
Dingo
Georgina

As we can see, it's copied the names from column K to column M. Not the most exciting thing to do, but we can use a similar technique to copy data from one sheet to another one or to another spreadsheet or even a completely different place like a Google Doc. So, you can start to see the power of this.

```
11:02:45 AM    Info         [Joan]
11:02:45 AM    Info         [Joan, Paula]
11:02:46 AM    Info         [Joan, Paula, Dingo]
11:02:46 AM    Info         [Joan, Paula, Dingo, Georgina]
```

The log clearly shows us what's happening, each time we go around the loop. It's adding one word at a time at the <u>end</u> of the array.

When we run the function, we can find out how long it took to run. Go to the menu on the left, and select Executions.

<>   Editor

⏰   Triggers

≡▶ Executions

This will show you all the times you've run functions in your code. It shows you how long the function took to complete and the status. Completed means it finished, but sometimes you might see Failed if there was a problem in script.

Function	Type	Start Time	Duration	Status
array5a	Editor	Mar 11, 2021, 10:55:55 AM	1.677 s	Completed

Here it took 1.677 seconds. It doesn't sound long, but as we'll see in a moment, this can be reduced. Normally, scripts have a maximum runtime limit of 6 minutes, so you can imagine a program of hundreds of lines long will mean every second counts. Plus, you want your program to run as quick as possible, as you don't want to sit there twiddling your thumbs while your program works its magic!

Reducing the execution time

The above code is fine and is useful in certain circumstances, but for the job we just did, that of copying one set of data and pasting it somewhere else, we can do it quicker.

```
85.   //Getting a range of values in one go and adding them to a sheet in one go
86.   //Note the different in execution time between array4a and 4b
87.   function array5b(){
88.     const ss = SpreadsheetApp.getActiveSpreadsheet().getActiveSheet();
```

We start off as before.

```
90.     const originalList2 = ss.getRange(1,11,4).getValues();
```

Line 90: Let's get the range of values in one go, by using the **getRange()** method which needs 3 arguments: start row, start column, number of rows, (as we're only getting 1 column, we don't need to get the number of columns). So, here we have row 1, column 11(K), 4 rows. Then get the values, as we saw in *array2*.

```
92.     Logger.log(originalList2);
93.
94.     ss.getRange(1,15,4).setValues(originalList2);
95.   }
```

Line 92: Let's log the content of the array. This isn't needed for the code to work.

Line 94: Then, we get the range we want to add the values to (column O) (remembering it has to have the same number of cells as the original data), then set the values from the variable *originalList2*.

O
Joan
Paula
Dingo
Georgina

As we can see, it added the 4 names.

Duration

0.787 s

Looking at the **executions**, we see it's much shorter than the previous example and due to that it is also quicker. It took only 0.787 seconds, over 2 times faster.

The difference being that in the previous example, we got a value and set it, then got another value and set it, etc, four times. Whereas, in this example, we got a group of values and set them in one go. You should always try to minimize the number of calls you're making, try to do things in one go to speed up your programs.

If you want to learn more about **arrays** visit the W3schools site:

https://www.w3schools.com/js/js_arrays.asp

https://www.w3schools.com/js/js_array_methods.asp

You can find the full piece of code for this chapter in Appendix 1.

CHAPTER 5 – If, Prompt, Menu & OnOpen Trigger

In this chapter, we're going to look at how we can get the computer to react to data in a spreadsheet and to user input. We're going to look at the following:

- Create your own menu in the spreadsheet to run your programs from
- **If**, **else if**, and **else** statements – to allow the program to make decisions
- Automatically set up the menu using the **onOpen** trigger
- Creating a dialogue box to allow the user to enter data using **ui.prompt**

Running scripts from the Script Editor is fine when you're writing them but you don't want your user to have to open the Script Editor every time they want to run your code. One of the best and easiest ways is to create a new menu in the spreadsheet. Here, we're going to add all the examples in this chapter to a single menu within our spreadsheet.

Creating new script file

Open the Script Editor from the Tools menu.

Tools   Add-ons   He

    ▦ Create a form

    ⌒ AppSheet

    <> Script editor

A script project can have more than one script file. As a general rule, for longer programs, it's a good idea to separate them into parts, as it's easier to find the part you want.

Let's create a new script file to put the menu code in. Click on the plus icon next to Files.

Files +

Code.gs

Then select Script.

Script

HTML

It will prompt you to name the script file.

Code.gs

Untitled

Type in a name. Here, I've called it "onOpen" just because the function will be called that, but you can call it whatever you like.

onOpen

Now you have two script files, the original default one called "Code" and the one we've just made "onOpen". ".gs" shows that they are script files.

Files

Code.gs

onOpen.gs

Rename the project, for example, "5menu".

Create a new spreadsheet menu

Click on the "Code" script file. Delete the code already in the editor.

```
1.  function onOpen() {
2.    SpreadsheetApp.getUi()
3.                 .createMenu('New menu')
4.                 .addItem('Example 1', 'example1')
5.                 .addItem('Example 2', 'example2')
6.                 .addItem('Example 3', 'example3')
7.                 .addItem('Example 4', 'example4')
8.                 .addItem('Example 5', 'example5')
9.                 .addItem('Example 6', 'example6')
10.                .addItem('Return to Sheet1', 'example6b')
11.                .addItem('Example 7', 'example7')
12.                .addItem('Example 8', 'example8')
13.                .addItem('Example 9', 'example9')
14.                .addToUi();
15. }
```

Line 1: Start with the function line and call it **onOpen()**. It has to be called this as this will tell the computer that you want this function to run every time the spreadsheet is opened. This is called a **trigger**.

Line 2: We need to get the spreadsheet's user-interface, so we use first the **SpreadsheetApp** class and then the method **getUi()**. Note, we don't add a semi-colon as most of the following lines are all connected to each other.

Line 3: Now, we need to create the menu and give it a name. Use the **createMenu()** method and in the brackets add the name of the menu you want in quote marks. Note, quote marks can be single or double ones but they must match.

Lines 4-13: Now, we add the items in our menu. So, logically we use the **addItem()** method for each one. In the brackets, you need to add the name of the item (i.e. what the user can see) and the name of the function that will be run when the user clicks on that name. There's one line per item.

Lines 14-15: Finally, we add it all to the user interface by using **addToUi()**. Note, as it's the last line we need to add the semi-colon. Then, we close the function with a curly bracket.

Run the function and you will see it's added a menu to the spreadsheet. Your very own menu!

New menu   Last edit
- Example 1
- Example 2
- Example 3
- Example 4
- Example 5
- Example 6
- Return to Sheet1
- Example 7
- Example 8
- Example 9

At the moment, clicking on the options won't do anything as we haven't written the functions for each one yet.

If statements (conditionals)

Example 1 – Set the background to red if the attendance is <80%

Here, we're going to start with a simple example to show the use of the **if statement**. We have the attendance figure for a student and we want to fill the cell red, if the attendance is less than the required 80% minimum.

	A	B
1	EXAMPLES 1-3 & 8	
2	Student	Attendance
3	John	75%

```
1. //Set background to red if attendance is less than 80%
2. function example1() {
3.     const ss = SpreadsheetApp.getActiveSheet();
4.     const cellB3 = ss.getRange("B3");
5.     const attendance = cellB3.getValue();
```

Line 2: Start with the function line.

Line 3: We need to get the current active sheet. We can do this directly from the **SpreadsheetApp** class by using **getActiveSheet()**. We'll then store that in the variable *ss*.

Line 4: Now, let's get the attendance figure. We do that by getting the range using **getRange()**, in this case just one cell, B3. We store this in the variable cellB3, as we will use this again later.

Line 5: Then we get the value of cell B3 using **getValue()**. We'll store it in the variable *attendance*.

Now we want to check if the attendance figure is less than 80% and if so, we'll fill the cell in red. We need an **if statement** for this and if you've used the IF function in spreadsheets before, you'll be familiar with this concept. If not, I'll explain it here.

If statements have the following structure:

If (a condition) {

   Do something if the condition is true

}

```
7.    if (attendance < 0.8) {
8.       cellB3.setBackground("red");
9.    }
10. }
```

Line 7: First, we start with the keyword **if** then in the brackets we put the condition we want to check for. In this case, it's if the figure in the attendance variable is less than 80% (or 0.8). Then we open the curly brackets.

Line 8: If this is true, we want to change the background colour to red. So, we use the range stored in the variable *cellB3* and set its background colour to red, using **setBackground()**.

Line 9: Close the if statement with a closed curly bracket.

Line 10: Close the function with another curly bracket.

Back on the spreadsheet, open the new menu and select Example 1. You'll have to authorize the script the first time. This will run the code and if the figure is less than 80% it will change the background to red.

EXAMPLES 1-3 & 8

Student	Attendance
John	75%

And sure enough, it has. The problem with this code is that it will only do something if the condition is true. So, if we changed the figure to 90% and ran it again, it wouldn't do anything as the condition is now false and we've not told it to do anything if the attendance is more than 80%, so the cell would remain red.

EXAMPLES 1-3 & 8

Student	Attendance
John	90%

Example 2 – Set the background to red if the attendance is <80% or otherwise green

This time let's adjust our code to do something if the condition isn't true.

```
12.   //Set background to red if attendance is less than 80%
13.   //Otherwise set it to green
14.   function example2() {
15.     const ss = SpreadsheetApp.getActiveSheet();
16.     const cellB3 = ss.getRange("B3");
17.     const attendance = cellB3.getValue();
```

Lines 14-17: Same as above, except call the function *example2*.

```
19.     if (attendance < 0.8) {
20.       cellB3.setBackground("red");
21.     }
```

Line 19-21: The **if** statement is the same as above.

```
23.     else {
24.       cellB3.setBackground("green");
25.     }
26.   }
```

This time we're going to add an **else** statement. This runs if the above **if** statement doesn't. It's like saying if the condition is not true, run this one.

Line 23: Here, we just need the **else** keyword, then open the curly brackets.

Line 24: Then, we state what we want it to do. In this case, we want it to change the background to green, if the attendance figure isn't less than 80% (i.e. is 80% or more).

Lines 25-26: Close the **else** statement with the curly bracket, and the function too.

EXAMPLES 1-3 & 8

Student	Attendance
John	90%

EXAMPLES 1-3 & 8

Student	Attendance
John	75%

Run the script and if you have a figure in B3 that's less than 80% the background will be red and if the figure is 80% or more it'll be green.

Example 3 – Set the background to red if the attendance is <70%, yellow 70-80%, green 80% or more

So, far we've only had 2 options but we can set up as many alternative options as we like by using the **else if** statement. In this example, let's have 3 attendance bands. Less than 70% it's red, 70% to 80% it's yellow, 80% or more it's green.

```
28.   //Set background to red if attendance is less than 70%
29.   //Set background to yellow if attendance is 70-80%
30.   //Set background to green if attendance is 80% or more
31.   function example3() {
32.     const ss = SpreadsheetApp.getActiveSheet();
33.     const cellB3 = ss.getRange("B3");
34.     const attendance = cellB3.getValue();
```

Lines 31-34: As before.

```
36.   if (attendance < 0.7) {
37.     cellB3.setBackground("red");
38.   }
```

Line 36: First, let's check if the attendance figure is less than 70%.

Lines 37-38: If so, it changes the background to red. Then close the **if** statement.

```
40.     else if (attendance < 0.8) {
41.        cellB3.setBackground("yellow");
42.     }
```

If the above isn't true then we want to check to see if it's less than 80%. Note, as we've already checked to see if it's less than 70% and it's not, really want we're doing here is checking that it's between 70% and 80%.

Line 40: As this is an alternative option we use **else if**. This works in the same way as the **if** statement.

Line 41: This time we change it to yellow if it's true.

```
44.     else {
45.        cellB3.setBackground("green");
46.     }
47.  }
```

Lines 44-47: Finally, if none of the above are true then we use the **else** function to run a default action, i.e. change it to green, as we now know it has to be 80% or more.

EXAMPLES 1-3 & 8

Student	Attendance
John	75%

Adding the figure 75% and running the code, we can see it's changed the background to yellow.

Example 4 – Set the background to red if the attendance is <80% OR the exam mark is <70%

Now, we have the situation where the student has to have attended more than 80% of classes and to get more than 70% in the exam to pass the course. So, we can think of it in another way, if he has less than 80% in attendance OR gets less than 70% in the exam, he won't pass and we need to highlight this name in red.

EXAMPLES 4-5

Student	Attendance	Exam
John	75%	80%

```
49.    //Set background of name to red if
50.    //attendance is less than 80% OR exam is less than 70%
51.    function example4() {
52.        const ss = SpreadsheetApp.getActiveSheet();
53.        const cellD3 = ss.getRange("D3");
54.        const attendance = ss.getRange("E3").getValue();
55.        const exam = ss.getRange("F3").getValue();
```

Lines 51-55: Similar to the examples before, we get cell D3, ready to add the appropriate colour, except this time we need the attendance figure from cell E3 and the exam mark from cell F3.

```
57.        if (attendance < 0.8 || exam < 0.7) {
58.            cellD3.setBackground("red");
59.        }
```

Lines 57-59: This time we're going to check for 2 different conditions and check if one is true or the other is true. We start with the attendance check then follow this by the 2 pipes || (normally found on the 1 key) then the exam check. This checks to see if the attendance is less than 80% OR if the exam mark is less than 70%. If either or both are true, it colours the student's name in cell D3 red.

```
61.        else {
62.            cellD3.setBackground("green");
63.        }
64.    }
```

Lines 61-64: As before, if the above isn't true, then we'll colour it green.

EXAMPLES 4-5

Student	Attendance	Exam
John	75%	80%

EXAMPLES 4-5

Student	Attendance	Exam
John	90%	80%

EXAMPLES 4-5

Student	Attendance	Exam
John	90%	60%

Example 5 – Set the background to green if the attendance is 80% or more AND the exam mark is 70% or more

We could look at the previous example from a different way and change the background to green, if both the attendance figure is 80% or more AND the exam mark is 70% or more.

D	E	F

EXAMPLES 4-5

Student	Attendance	Exam
John	75%	80%

```
66.  //Set background of name to green if
67.  //attendance is 80% or more AND exam is 70% or more
68.  function example5() {
69.    const ss = SpreadsheetApp.getActiveSheet();
70.    const cellD3 = ss.getRange("D3");
71.    const attendance = ss.getRange("E3").getValue();
72.    const exam = ss.getRange("F3").getValue();
```

Lines 68-72: As before.

```
74.    if (attendance >= 0.8 && exam >= 0.7) {
75.      cellD3.setBackground("green");
76.    }
```

Lines 74-76: Again, we will check for two conditions, but this time we want to know if both are true. We start with the attendance check (80% or more) then follow it by the 2 ampersands **&&**, which mean AND. Then, we add the exam check. If both of these are true we change the cell colour to green.

```
78.    else {
79.      cellD3.setBackground("red");
80.    }
81.  }
```

Lines 78-81: If at least one of them isn't true then it runs the **else** statement and fills the colour red.

EXAMPLES 4-5

Student	Attendance	Exam
John	90%	60%

Example 6 – Get the students' data and add it to their individual sheet

Now we've looked at the basics of **if**, **else if**, and **else**, let's look at how we can use the input from a user and get the program to act accordingly based on that input. Here, we have a sheet with the attendance and exam marks for 4 students. What I'd like the program to do is when I type in the student's name in cell B5 and I run the program, it will get their data and write it on their individual sheet.

5		Name: Ringo	EXAMPLE 6		
6					
7	**John**	Jan	Feb	Mar	Apr
8	Attendance	75%	60%	70%	80%
9	Exam	60%	65%	65%	70%
10	**Ringo**	Jan	Feb	Mar	Apr
11	Attendance	50%	60%	70%	70%
12	Exam	50%	80%	70%	50%
13	**Paul**	Jan	Feb	Mar	Apr
14	Attendance	85%	90%	95%	100%
15	Exam	60%	65%	65%	70%
16	**George**	Jan	Feb	Mar	Apr
17	Attendance	85%	50%	90%	90%
18	Exam	90%	95%	80%	85%

This time as we'll be using multiple sheets, let's be specific about which sheets we're using. Using just **getActiveSheet()** may cause problems if we haven't got the right sheet open.

```
83.    //Open sheet from name in cell B5 and paste student's data
84.    function example6() {
85.        const ss = SpreadsheetApp.getActiveSpreadsheet();
86.        const sheet1 = ss.getSheetByName('Sheet1');
87.        const name = sheet1.getRange("B5").getValue();
```

Line 85: First, let's get the active spreadsheet and add it to the variable *ss*.

Line 86: Then, let's get the sheet called *Sheet1* by its name by using **getSheetByName()**.

Line 87: Then, we get the student's name on *sheet1* from cell B5 and store it in the variable *name*.

```
89.    if(name === "John") {
90.        var figures = sheet1.getRange("A7:E9").getValues();
91.    }
```

We're going to check the name the user's entered in cell B5 is equal to one of the 4 students we have in our table. Then it will get the corresponding data for that student.

Line 89: First, we check if the name is the same as "John". Note, the use of the triple equals sign to mean equals to. One common mistake is to write a single one here, which is want is used to assign a value, for example, to assign it to a variable.

Line 90: If it is "John", then we get John's data from the range A7 to E9 and store it in the *figures* variable. Note, we need to use **var** here as we will be using the variable outside this if statement, so outside this scope. So, **let** or **const** wouldn't work as they wouldn't be "seen" or defined.

```
93.    else if(name === "Ringo") {
94.        var figures = sheet1.getRange("A10:E12").getValues();
95.    }
96.
97.    else if(name === "Paul") {
98.        var figures = sheet1.getRange("A13:E15").getValues();
99.    }
100.
101.   else if(name === "George") {
102.       var figures = sheet1.getRange("A16:E18").getValues();
103.   }
```

We do the same for each of the students but here we use **else if** as these are alternatives to the first **if** statement. For each student, we just change the range. Whatever name is chosen the appropriate figures are added to the *figures* variable.

Assuming we've written one of the 4 names, we have the student's name (stored in *name*) and the data (stored in *figures*), we need to add it to their individual sheet.

```
105.   const studentSheet = ss.getSheetByName(name).activate();
106.   studentSheet.getRange("A1:E3").setValues(figures);
107. }
```

Line 105: First, we need to get the sheet we want. We do this by getting the sheet by its name. The name will depend on the one which the user typed in, which is stored in the variable *name*. I've added the **active()** method so that it opens that sheet.

Line 106: Finally, we add the data from Sheet1 to the student's sheet. We get the student's sheet, get the range we want (note the size of the range must match the size of the original range) and then we use **setValues()** to add the values to the student's sheet in one go.

Run the code and you will see the student's sheet open and the following data added. As you can see it's not formatted. It's important to remember that when we use **getValues()** we are only getting the values, and not any of the formatting. We would have to set the formatting to make it look a bit prettier or to format the student sheets beforehand.

	A	B	C	D	E
1	Ringo	Jan	Feb	Mar	Apr
2	Attendance	0.5	0.6	0.7	0.7
3	Exam	0.5	0.8	0.7	0.5

Example 6B – Return back to the first sheet

Having a code which takes us to a specific sheet is great, but what happens when we want to go back to the original sheet? This little piece of code does just that.

```
109. //Return back to Sheet1
110. function example6b() {
111.     const ss = SpreadsheetApp.getActiveSpreadsheet();
112.     const sheet1 = ss.getSheetByName('Sheet1').activate();
113. }
```

Lines 110-113: The key line here is to get the sheet called Sheet1 and to open it. In the menu on the spreadsheet, I've called this "Return to Sheet1".

Example 7 – Ask for the student's name, then open their individual sheet

In all the examples above, we've used data in the spreadsheet as the input. Now, let's make this a little bit more professional. Let's open a dialogue box where the user will enter the student's name they want and to keep it simple, let's just open that student's sheet. You could of course, adapt the code from the previous example, to add the data to the sheet.

```
115. //Ask which sheet user wants to open and then open it
116. function example7() {
117.   const ss = SpreadsheetApp.getActiveSpreadsheet();
118.   const ui = SpreadsheetApp.getUi();
119.   const response = ui.prompt('Enter name:');
```

Line 118: As with the creating the menu, we first need to get the user interface, using the **getUi()** method, then store it in the variable *ui*.

Line 119: Then, we use the **prompt()** method to display a dialogue box which will require the user to enter something. In the brackets, we add the text we want to show in the box. The prompt we'll store in the variable *response*.

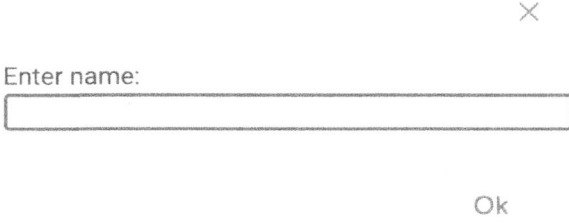

The user has 2 options, either they type something in and click OK or they could just close the dialogue box without entering anything.

```
121.   if (response.getSelectedButton() === ui.Button.OK) {
122.     const name = response.getResponseText();
123.     ss.getSheetByName(name).activate();
124.   }
125. }
```

Line 121: First, we check to see if they have clicked the OK button. We get the prompt which is stored in *response* and get the button that was selected by using **getSelectedButton()**. Then, we check to see if this is the same as the OK button by getting the OK button in the user interface by using **ui.Button.OK**.

Line 122: If it is the OK button, then we get the name that was added in the box by the user. We do this by getting the response text using **getResponseText()** and we store this in the variable *name*.

Line 123: Then, we open the sheet with the name stored in the variable *name*, by using **getSheetbyName()** and **activate()**.

Lines 124-125: Close the **if** statement and function.

Here, I haven't used an **else** statement, as if they just close the dialogue box, I don't want anything to happen, so an else statement isn't needed.

Running the code, we will see the dialogue box open prompting us for a name.

Enter a name and click OK and this will take us to that student's sheet.

One problem with this code is that if the user enters a name that doesn't match one of the 4 students, it will throw an error.

Example 8 – Set the background to red if the attendance is <80% otherwise green (ternary operator)

Referring back to example2, we could simplify the code a little by using an alternative way to deal with a condition that is either true or false. It's called the **ternary operator** and instead of writing 6 lines of code we can do it in just 1.

We want to check if John's attendance is less than 80% and if so, change the background to red and if not change it to green.

	A	B
1	EXAMPLES 1-3 & 8	
2	Student	Attendance
3	John	75%

```
127. //Using ternary operator-If less than 80% set background red, otherwise
     green
128. function example8() {
129.    const ss = SpreadsheetApp.getActiveSheet();
130.    const cellB3 = ss.getRange("B3");
131.    const attendance = cellB3.getValue();
132.    (attendance < 0.8) ?
        cellB3.setBackground("red"):cellB3.setBackground("green");
133. }
```

Line 129: We get the active sheet (make sure you have *Sheet1* open when running this).

Line 130: We get the cell B3 and store it in the variable *cellB3*.

Line 131: Then, get the attendance figure in that cell.

This has the following format:

(condition to check) ? action to take if it's true : action to take if it's false;

Line 132: We check if the attendance figure is less than 80%, then there's the question mark. Then we state we want to change the background to red if it's true. Then a colon, then we want to change the background to green if it's false.

As we can see it does exactly the same as example 2 but with less code:

EXAMPLES 1-3 & 8	
Student	Attendance
John	75%

To simplify the line even further, you could also write this with the following syntax:

cellB3.setBackground((attendance < 0.8) ? "red":"green"))

I.e. put the ternary conditional in the method setBackground's brackets.

Example 9 – Set the background colour for all students' attendance figures

Writing code for just one student is not really a good use of Apps Script and using Sheet's Conditional Formatting would be far better. The next could also be done using conditional formatting, but we're here to learn Apps Script right? And here we're going to combine a **for loop** with the **if** statements, so consolidating the learning from the previous chapter on loops.

Here, we have a table of students' attendance figures and we're going to add red, yellow, or green depending on the figure for each.

H	I
EXAMPLE 9	

Student	Attendance
John	75%
Ringo	70%
Paul	60%
George	85%

```
135. //Set background colour for all students' attendance figures
136. function example9() {
137.   const ss = SpreadsheetApp.getActiveSpreadsheet();
138.   const sheet1 = ss.getSheetByName('Sheet1');
139.   const attendanceFigures = sheet1.getRange("I3:I6").getValues();
```

Line 138: First, get the sheet called *Sheet1*.

Line 139: Then get the range I3 to I6. As there is more than one value, we use **getValues()**. Then we store it in the variable *attendanceFigures*.

```
141.   for (i=0;i<attendanceFigures.length;i++){
```

In the array *attendanceFigures*, in index 0, we have the value from cell I2; in index 1 from value from I3, and so on.

Line 141: Set up the **for loop** and we want to go from 0 (the first value in the array).

We want the loop to continue until the end of the range, i.e. I5 (index 3 in the array). We could state that it continues while i<4, but the code can easily work out how many figures are in the array, by getting its length, using the **length** property. So, **attendanceFigures.length** = 4.

Then, we want to move down the rows one at a time, so we increase *i* by 1 each time using *i++*.

```
143.        let r = i+3;
144.        let rangeToChangeColour = sheet1.getRange(r,9);
```

Line 143: We're going to need the row number, and we can get it by linking it to the array index. So, array index 0 is row 3 (I3), so let's make the variable *r* 3 more than the variable *i*, which is the array index.

Line 144: We get the cell we're currently looping on, so this will start on row 3 and column 9 (i.e. I3) and go to row 6 and column 9. (I6).

```
146.        if (attendanceFigures[i] < 0.7) {
147.            rangeToChangeColour.setBackground("red");
148.        }
```

Then within the curly brackets, we carry out the **if** checks.

Line 146: We check if the figure in *attendanceFigures* is less than 70%. The first time around the loop it will check if the attendance figure in cell I2 is <70%, as i = 0, and so on.

Line 147: If it is <70%, then it gets the range and changes the background to red. The range (row, column) will be (*r*, 9), as for example, we are starting in row 3 (I3) and we are in column 9, as it's column I.

```
150.        else if (attendanceFigures[i] < 0.8) {
151.            rangeToChangeColour.setBackground("yellow");
152.        }
```

We then check if the attendance is less than 80%, using the else **if** statement.

```
154.        else {
155.            rangeToChangeColour.setBackground("green");
156.        }
157.    }
158. }
```

Lines 154-155: Finally, if it's neither less than 70% or 80% it must be 80% or more, so we change the background to green.

Lines 156-158: We close the else statement, for loop, and function with the curly brackets.

Run the code and you will see it has filled the cells in the appropriate colours.

EXAMPLE 9

Student	Attendance
John	75%
Ringo	70%
Paul	60%
George	85%

If you want to learn more about **if, else if, else** or **logical operators** visit the W3schools site:

https://www.w3schools.com/js/js_operators.asp

https://www.w3schools.com/js/js_if_else.asp

Plus, more information on menus and the user interface (dialogue boxes, etc), visit the Google developers site:

https://developers.google.com/apps-script/reference/base/menu

https://developers.google.com/apps-script/reference/base/ui

You can find the full piece of code for this chapter in Appendix 1.

CHAPTER 6 – SpreadsheetApp & the For In Loop

In this chapter, we're going to look at the Google Workspace services, the Google documentation that's available to help you, and then focus on one particular area, **SpreadsheetApp** to then create some spreadsheets. Plus, we're also going to see the really useful **for in loop** in action.

It's important to have an understanding of how the different parts of Apps Script fit together. So, first let's go to the Google documentation, which can be found at:

https://developers.google.com/apps-script/reference/spreadsheet/

On the left of the web page, there is a list of the Google Workspace services available. As you can see in the list below, we can work directly with most of the main apps within Google Workspace, from calendars to spreadsheets. As your codes get more complex, you will start working with various services at the same time. So, for example, we could have data in a spreadsheet and create a Google Doc from it, or we could use that data to create a Google Form and to create an event on the calendar.

Google Workspace Services

Google Workspace services
- Calendar
- Contacts
- Data Studio
- Document
- Domain
- Drive
- Forms
- Gmail
- Groups
- Language
- Maps
- Sites
- Slides
- Spreadsheet

Advanced Google services

Script Services

Spreadsheet Service

In this chapter, we're going to focus on the Spreadsheet service, which will provide an example as to how all this works together. As we can see from the description below, the Spreadsheet service allows us to work with Google Sheets.

Spreadsheet Service 🔖   Send feedback

This service allows scripts to create, access, and modify Google Sheets files. See also the guide to storing data in spreadsheets.

Under the **Service**, we have the **Classes**. These are basically sub categories of the service. The first time you look at the list below, the number of different classes scares you a little and you wonder where to start! But when you start looking at the details, it's not that difficult.

Classes

Name	Brief description
`AutoFillSeries`	An enumeration of the types of series used to calculate auto-filled values.
`Banding`	Access and modify bandings, the color patterns applied to rows or columns of a range.
`BandingTheme`	An enumeration of banding themes.
`BigQueryDataSourceSpec`	Access the existing BigQuery data source specification.
`BigQueryDataSourceSpecBuilder`	The builder for `BigQueryDataSourceSpecBuilder`.
`BooleanCondition`	Access boolean conditions in `ConditionalFormatRules`.
`BooleanCriteria`	An enumeration representing the boolean criteria that can be used in conditional format or filter.
`BorderStyle`	Styles that can be set on a range using `Range.setBorder(top, left, bottom, right, vertical, horizontal, color, style)`.
`Color`	A representation for a color.

The main four you will use time and time again are near the bottom of the list: Range, Sheet, Spreadsheet, SpreadsheetApp.

`Range`	Access and modify spreadsheet ranges.
`RangeList`	A collection of one or more `Range` instances in the same sheet.
`RecalculationInterval`	An enumeration representing the possible intervals used in spreadsheet recalculation.
`RelativeDate`	An enumeration representing the relative date options for calculating a value to be used in date-based `BooleanCriteria`.
`RichTextValue`	A stylized text string used to represent cell text.
`RichTextValueBuilder`	A builder for Rich Text values.
`Selection`	Access the current active selection n the active sheet.
`Sheet`	Access and modify spreadsheet sheets.
`SheetType`	The different types of sheets that can exist in a spreadsheet.
`Slicer`	Represents a slicer, which is used to filter ranges, charts and pivot tables in a non-collaborative manner.
`SortOrder`	An enumeration representing the sort order.
`SortSpec`	The sorting specification.
`Spreadsheet`	Access and modify Google Sheets files.
`SpreadsheetApp`	Access and create Google Sheets files.

There is a hierarchy to these:

SpreadsheetApp > Spreadsheet > Sheet > Range

In general terms, if you want to edit some cells in a spreadsheet, you need to tell the code which spreadsheet you're working with, which sheet you want to edit, and then which range.

In the upcoming chapters we're going to look at all of these but for now let's focus on just the first of those classes, **SpreadsheetApp**. On the menu on the left of the web page, click on **Spreadsheet** (if not already open) and **SpreadsheetApp**.

SpreadsheetApp

- ▼ Spreadsheet
    - Overview
        - SpreadsheetApp

This will open the documentation for the **SpreadsheetApp**. As we can see from the description below, this class is mainly for creating and opening Google Sheets.

Class SpreadsheetApp

Access and create Google Sheets files. This class is the parent class for the Spreadsheet service.

Underneath **classes** we have **methods**. These are the specific instructions that tell the program to do a specific job within that **class**.

Methods

Method	Return type	Brief description
`create(name)`	Spreadsheet	Creates a new spreadsheet with the given name.
`create(name, rows, columns)`	Spreadsheet	Creates a new spreadsheet with the given name and the specified number of rows and columns.
`enableAllDataSourcesExecution()`	void	Enables data execution for all types of data sources.
`enableBigQueryExecution()`	void	Enables data execution for BigQuery data source.
`flush()`	void	Applies all pending Spreadsheet changes.
`getActive()`	Spreadsheet	Returns the currently active spreadsheet, or `null` if there is none.

On the right of the page (see list below), we can see a list of the **methods** available under the **SpreadsheetApp** class. The names of them usually give a good indication as to what they do. If you want to jump to information about a particular method, just click on the method in this list and it will take you to the information for that method.

Table of contents

Properties

Methods

Detailed documentation

  create(name)

  create(name, rows, columns)

  enableAllDataSourcesExecution()

  enableBigQueryExecution()

  flush()

  getActive()

  getActiveRange()

  getActiveRangeList()

  getActiveSheet()

  getActiveSpreadsheet()

Let's click on the **create(name)** method.

Methods

Method	Return type	Brief description
create(name)	Spreadsheet	Creates a new spreadsheet with the given name.

Sometimes, it gives you an example showing how to use it. For example, here we can see that we need to use the **SpreadsheetApp** then add the create method to it and give it a name in the brackets.

`create(name)`

Creates a new spreadsheet with the given name.

```
// The code below creates a new spreadsheet "Finances" and logs the URL for it
var ssNew = SpreadsheetApp.create("Finances");
Logger.log(ssNew.getUrl());
```

It states the parameters it needs. So in this case, it needs a name in the form of a string, e.g. a piece of text.

Parameters

Name	Type	Description
name	String	The name for the spreadsheet.

It also states what will be returned when the method is used. So, here a new spreadsheet will be created.

Return

`Spreadsheet` — a new spreadsheet

At the end, it will also state what authorization is required. For what we will be doing in this book, you will just need to authorize the script as we've been doing, and just that.

Authorization

Scripts that use this method require authorization with one or more of the following scopes:

- `https://www.googleapis.com/auth/spreadsheets.currentonly`
- `https://www.googleapis.com/auth/spreadsheets`

OK, so now we have an overview of **services**, **classes**, and **methods**, let's jump in and work our way through some examples, showing how the **SpreadsheetApp** works.

Creating menu – SpreadsheetApp.getUi()

First, let's create a menu to allow us to run all the examples from it without having to go back to the script editor every time. Conveniently, this will also show one of the methods linked to the **SpreadsheetApp** class. We saw the **onOpen** trigger in the last chapter, so this should be familiar to you now. I'm going to create a new script file for it and put it in there to keep it separate from the main set of functions, like we saw in an earlier chapter.

```
1.  //Create menu to run examples from
2.  function onOpen(){
3.    SpreadsheetApp.getUi()
4.      .createMenu("Examples")
5.      .addItem("example 1", "example1")
```

```
6.       .addItem("example 2", "example2")
7.       .addItem("example 3", "example3")
8.       .addItem("example 4", "example4")
9.       .addItem("example 5", "example5")
10.      .addItem("example 6", "example6")
11.      .addItem("example 7", "example7")
12.      .addToUi();
13. }
```

Line 2: Use the name **onOpen()** to trigger it to run when the user opens the spreadsheet.

Line 3: Here, we use the **SpreadsheetApp** class and the **getUi()** method as we're editing the user interface of the spreadsheet.

Line 4: We create a menu using **createMenu()** and give it a name.

Lines 5-11: Then, we add the items in the menu using **additem()**. In the brackets add, the name of the items and the function names they correspond with.

Lines 12-13: Finally, we add all this to the UI using **addToUi()** and end it with a semi-colon and close the function with a curly bracket.

It's useful to store this chunk of code in a separate script file, as you'll probably be using it for various projects, so you'll want to just copy and paste it in and then edit it to save you time. Appendix 2 shows you how to create a standalone script file and how to add the Script Editor to your Google Drive.

Global Variables / variables

In some of the following examples we're going to be using the same spreadsheet and the same sheet, so instead of repeating the code in various examples, we can write them outside the functions, so that the same code can be used in different functions. These are called **global variables** or **variables** and this just means that the variables or variables are available to all the functions in this script project, not just within a particular function as is often the case. So, we're going to set up two variables, one for the active spreadsheet and one for the active sheet.

Note, global variables/variables should be written in capital letters to clearly show that they are global ones.

```
1. //Global variables
2. const SS = SpreadsheetApp.getActiveSpreadsheet();
3. const SHEET = SS.getActiveSheet();
```

Line 2: Get the active spreadsheet using the **SpreadsheetApp** class and the **getActiveSpreadsheet()** method and store it in the variable *SS*.

Line 3: Get the active sheet from the variable we just set up, *SS*, along with **getActiveSheet()** and store it in the variable *SHEET*.

Example 1 – Creating a new spreadsheet

Let's start with an easy example. We're going to create a new spreadsheet and call it "New Spreadsheet1".

Method	Return type	Brief description
create(name)	Spreadsheet	Creates a new spreadsheet with the given name.

```
5. //Create a new spreadsheet
6. function example1() {
7.    SpreadsheetApp.create("New Spreadsheet1");
8. }
```

Line 6: Set up the function and call it *example1*.

Lines 7-8: Start with **SpreadsheetApp** then use the **create()** method to make a new spreadsheet. In the brackets, add the name you want to give the file. Then close the function.

Run the function example1 and we can see in our My Drive, the newly-created spreadsheet:

New Spreadsheet1

Example 2 – Creating a spreadsheet with limited rows and columns

We're going to create another spreadsheet but this time we're going to add some extra information in the brackets to set it up with a fixed number of rows and columns.

create(name, rows, columns)	Spreadsheet	Creates a new spreadsheet with the given name and the specified number of rows and columns.

```
10.  //Create a new spreadsheet with 20 rows and 10 columns
11.  function example2() {
12.    SpreadsheetApp.create("New Spreadsheet2", 20, 10);
13.  }
```

Line 11: Set up the function called *example2*.

Line 12: We again use the **create()** method, but this time there are 3 pieces of information within the brackets: spreadsheet name, number of rows, number of columns.

As we can see it created a spreadsheet as before.

New Spreadsheet2

And we have set it up with a fixed number of rows and columns in it.

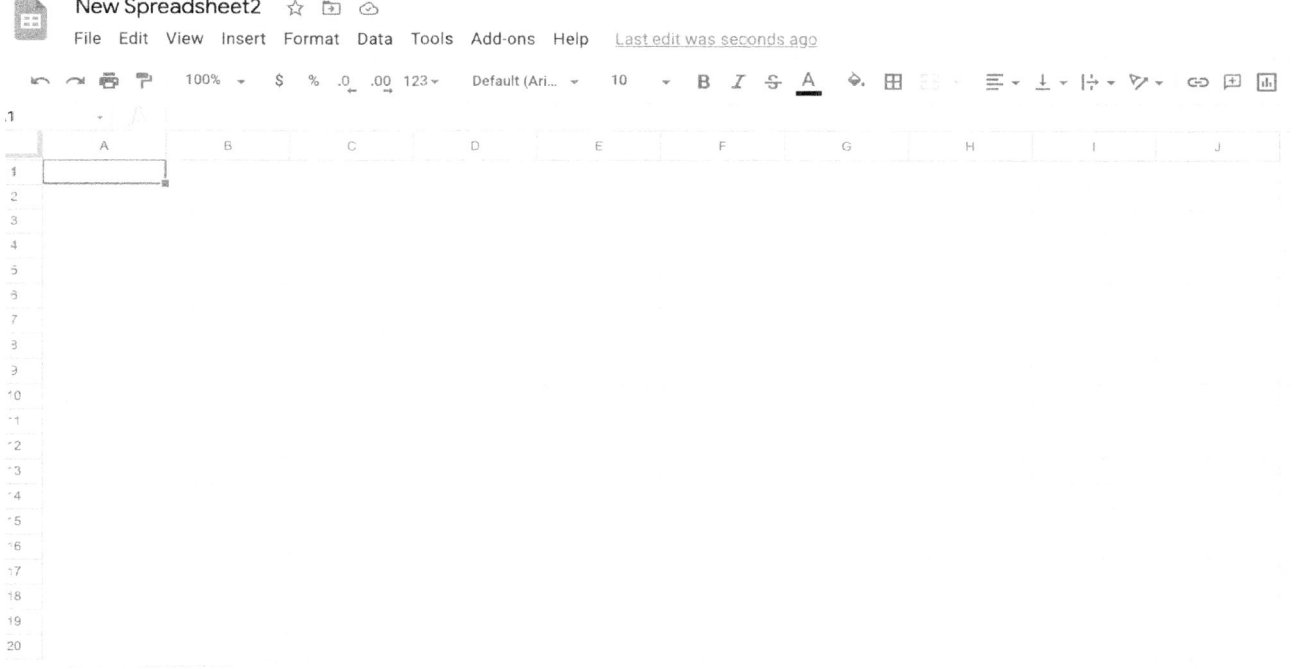

Example 3 – Creating a spreadsheet with a name from the sheet

Quite often the name we want to give the newly-created spreadsheet is taken from some source of data. Here, we're going to get the name of the spreadsheet from one of the cells in the original spreadsheet.

```
15.  //Create a new spreadsheet with a name from a sheet
16.  function example3() {
17.    const name = SHEET.getRange("A1").getValue();
18.    SpreadsheetApp.create(name);
19.  }
```

Line 16: Set up the function *example3*.

Line 17: First, we need to get the name from the cell on the sheet. Get the sheet (from the global variable *SHEET* we set up earlier), get cell A1 using **getRange()** and get its value using **getValue()**. Then, we store it in the variable *name*.

	A
1	New Spreadsheet 3

Line 18: Then, we use the **create()** method we used before, but this time use the variable *name* in the brackets.

As we can see, it has named the new spreadsheet with the name from cell A1.

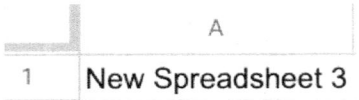 New Spreadsheet 3

Example 4 – Creating multiple spreadsheets with different names

This time let's take it a step further and create 3 different spreadsheets using names from the original sheet. We'll use a **for in loop** to make the different spreadsheets.

```
21.  //Create multiple spreadsheets with different names from a sheet
22.  function example4() {
23.    const names = SHEET.getRange("B1:B3").getValues();
```

B
New Spreadsheet 4a
New Spreadsheet 4b
New Spreadsheet 4c

Line 23: First, we get the names of the spreadsheets from the sheet. These are stored in cells B1 to B3. As there is more than 1 name, we use **getValues()** to store the names in an array and we'll call that array *names*. Here's what the content of that array looks like:

```
[[New Spreadsheet 4a], [New Spreadsheet 4b], [New Spreadsheet 4c]]
```

Now, we start the **for in loop**. The beauty of the **for in loop** is that it will automatically work out how many items are in your array and loop that many times around. So, in our *names* array we have 3 names, so it will go around the loop 3 times, and do whatever we put in between the curly brackets, 3 times. I.e. in this case, it will create 3 different spreadsheets.

The syntax for a **for in loop** is:

for (counter variable **in** array name**) {**

   Do something x the number of items in the array

}

```
24.    for (i in names){
25.       SpreadsheetApp.create(names[i]);
26.    }
27. }
```

Line 24: Here, we'll use *i* as the counter and we add *names* as it's the array we want to loop through.

Line 25: Each loop we want to create a spreadsheet, so we use the **SpreadsheetApp** and **create()** as before. This time in the brackets, we refer to the information in the array *name* and we need to move position within that array each time we go around. So, the first name will be at position 0 (*name*[0]), then position 1 (*name*[1]), and so on. The counter *i* automatically starts at 0.

Lines 26-27: Then we close the loop and the function.

As we can see in our My Drive, it's created the 3 spreadsheets and given each one a different name, which has been taken from the cells B1 to B3 in our original sheet. All with very few lines of code!

- New Spreadsheet 4a

- New Spreadsheet 4b

- New Spreadsheet 4c

Example 5 – Getting data from one spreadsheet and adding it to another (URL)

Here, we're going to see how easy it is to get data from one spreadsheet and to add it to another spreadsheet.

`openByUrl(url)`	Spreadsheet	Opens the spreadsheet with the given URL.

```
29.  //Get a value from one spreadsheet and add it into another, using its URL
30.  function example5(){
31.    const text = SHEET.getRange("C1").getValue();
```

Line 31: First, we need to get the text in cell C1 in the first spreadsheet.

Use **getRange()** and **getValue()** to get that, using the global variable *SHEET* again. Then store it in the variable *text*.

```
32.    const newSS =
   SpreadsheetApp.openByUrl("https://docs.google.com/spreadsheets/d/1xFwNEaBjvH
   eBfxW_z4wBsyozedn5sQ82FWsiv-J5aEI/edit#gid=0");
33.    newSS.getActiveSheet().getRange("A1").setValue(text);
34.  }
```

Line 32: Now, we need to get the other spreadsheet. We do that by 'opening' it. Note, this doesn't open it for the user but it does on the server-side and tells the code that we are now working with this new spreadsheet. Here, we're going to open it by its URL. So, use the **openByUrl()** method and add the complete URL in the brackets between quote marks. Store the spreadsheet in *newSS*. Add your own URL here.

Line 33: We then use *newSS* to tell the code that's the spreadsheet we want to use, then we get the active sheet and add the text using **getRange()** and **setValue()**. This will add the text in cell A1 in our new spreadsheet.

Example5 - Second spreadsheet

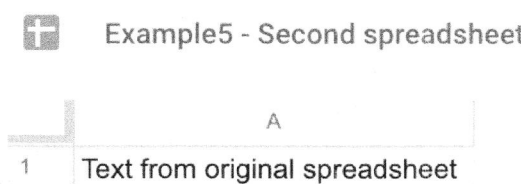

Example 6 – Getting data from one spreadsheet and adding it to another (ID)

This is very similar to the previous example but this time we're going to use the ID of the new spreadsheet and not the URL. The ID is the part with random looking letters and numbers after the /d/ and before the /edit parts.

`openById(id)`   Spreadsheet   Opens the spreadsheet with the given ID.

```
36.  //Get a value from one spreadsheet and add it into another, using it ID
37.  function example6(){
38.    const text = SHEET.getRange("C1").getValue();
39.    const newSS =
    SpreadsheetApp.openById("1xFwNEaBjvHeBfxW_z4wBsyozedn5sQ82FWsiv-J5aEI");
40.    newSS.getActiveSheet().getRange("A2").setValue(text);
41.  }
```

As we can see, in cell A2 it's added the text from the original spreacsheet. The text in cell A1 is from the previous example.

	A
1	Text from original spreadsheet
2	Text from original spreadsheet

Example 7 – Creating multiple spreadsheets with different names and different pieces of text

Finally, let's create 3 different spreadsheets each with its own name, which we will get from our original sheet. Plus, we will add a different piece of text in each one. This is just an expansion of what we've seen so far and you'll see it's really easy to do.

	D	E
	Example 7-Spreadsheet A	Text for spreadsheet A
	Example 7-Spreadsheet B	Text for spreadsheet B
	Example 7-Spreadsheet C	Text for spreadsheet C

```
43.  //Create multiple spreadsheets with different names and pieces of text from
     a sheet
44.  function example7(){
45.    const ssNames = SHEET.getRange("D1:D3").getValues(),
46.          texts = SHEET.getRange("E1:E3").getValues();
```

Line 45: First, let's get the list of spreadsheet names from cells D1 to D3 and store it in the array *ssNames*.

Note, here I've ended the line with a comma and not a semi-colon. I've done that as the next line will also be a variable, and we don't have to type in **const** again, we just add the variable name, then at the end of that line add the semi-colon. This leads to cleaner code and saves a bit of typing.

Line 46: Get the list of texts from column E that we're going to add into the spreadsheets and store them in the variable *texts*.

```
48.    for (i in ssNames){
49.      let spreadsheet = SpreadsheetApp.create(ssNames[i]);
50.      spreadsheet.getActiveSheet().getRange("A1").setValue(texts[i]);
51.    }
52.  }
```

Line 48: We're going to loop down the both lists so let's set up a **for in loop.** As both our lists are the same length, we can just use one of them to count the number of times we go around the loop. Here, we're using the *ssNames* array.

Line 49: First, we want to create the spreadsheets and give it a name from the array ssNames. As before, we control which name we're using by the counter i. So, for example, spreadsheet 1 will use the first name in the array. We store the spreadsheet in the variable *spreadsheet*.

Line 50: Then, we call that spreadsheet and get its active sheet and cell A1, and add the text from the text array at the current position. So, for example, in spreadsheet 1, we'll use the first piece of text.

As we can see, it's created the 3 different spreadsheets, given them individual names, and added a different piece of text in each one.

📄 Example 7-Spreadsheet A

📄 Example 7-Spreadsheet B

📄 Example 7-Spreadsheet C

	A
1	Text for spreadsheet A

	A
1	Text for spreadsheet B

	A
1	Text for spreadsheet C

If you want to learn more about **for in loops** visit the W3schools site:

https://www.w3schools.com/jsref/jsref_forin.asp

Plus, find more information on the **SpreadsheetApp** here:

https://developers.google.com/apps-script/reference/spreadsheet/spreadsheet-app

You can find the full piece of code for this chapter in Appendix 1.

CHAPTER 7 – Spreadsheet Class

In the last chapter, we looked at the **SpreadsheetApp** class. Now, let's look at the next group related to spreadsheets, which is the **Spreadsheet** class. This class allows us to:

- copy spreadsheets
- work with sheets, such as moving, inserting, and deleting them
- add or remove collaborators to the spreadsheet
- display messages, in the form of the toast message

Class Spreadsheet

Access and modify Google Sheets files. Common operations are adding new sheets and adding collaborators.

Go to the Google documentation:

https://developers.google.com/apps-script/reference/spreadsheet/spreadsheet

and you'll see all the methods available to the Spreadsheet class.

Table of contents

Methods

Deprecated methods

Detailed documentation

　addDeveloperMetadata(key)

　addDeveloperMetadata(key, visibility)

　addDeveloperMetadata(key, value)

　addDeveloperMetadata(key, value, visibility)

　addEditor(emailAddress)

　addEditor(user)

　addEditors(emailAddresses)

　addMenu(name, subMenus)

You will see that there are a lot of methods available but in fact, there are many that can be found in the **Sheet class** too, which I'll cover in the next chapter. So, here I'm going to focus on the most common ones, which are unique to the **Spreadsheet class**.

Example 1 – Copying and renaming a spreadsheet and using the Toast message

To start, let's make a copy of a spreadsheet and rename it by getting the name of the original spreadsheet and adding to it. Then, we'll let the user know the process has finished by displaying a message in the original spreadsheet.

```
1.  //Copy a spreadsheet, rename the new one using original name
2.  //Display a toast message once the process has finished
3.  function example1() {
4.    const ss1 = SpreadsheetApp.getActiveSpreadsheet(),
5.          ss1Name = ss1.getName();
6.    ss1.copy(ss1Name + "-example1");
7.    ss1.toast("Spreadsheet copied & named", "Finished", 5);
8.  }
```

Line 3: Set up the function and call it *example1*.

Line 4: First, I want to make a copy of the current spreadsheet that's open (i.e. the active one) so we use **getActiveSpreadsheet()** to get it and we store it in the variable *ss1*. Note, I've added a comma on the end to add another variable on the next line.

Line 5: As we're going to use the name of this spreadsheet, we need to get its name. So, we use the variable *ss1* and then use **getName()**. We then store it in the variable *ss1Name*.

Line 6: Now, let's copy the original spreadsheet and we put the name of the new spreadsheet in the brackets. We're going to name it using a combination of the original spreadsheet's name and add "-example1" at the end. So, we state the variable *ss1Name*, use a plus sign to join the two parts together and then in quote marks add the text we want.

Line 7: Finally, let's let the user know that the spreadsheet has been copied and named using the toast message. As we are working in the original spreadsheet, we get the variable *ss1* and then add **toast()** to it. In the brackets, we add the parameters we want. Here, I'm using the toast message option which allows us to add a message, a title, and state how many seconds the message will be displayed for.

Toast messages, as you'll see, are messages that pop up from the bottom right-hand corner, like toast in a toaster. I often use them, either as a message to show the user the progress of the process, if it's a particularly long one, or just to let them know when everything is finished.

The good things are that the message doesn't stop the code working in the background, so doesn't delay it, and it doesn't require user interaction like an alert message would.

Run the code. For this example, as soon as you've clicked the play button to run the code, open the spreadsheet. When the code has come near the end, you'll see the toast message pop up in the right-hand corner of the screen.

Finished
Spreadsheet copied & named

In your My Drive, you'll see the newly-copied spreadsheet, with the name we set up.

7-Spreadsheet-example1

Example 2 – Adding editors or viewers to a spreadsheet

When creating a new spreadsheet, we sometimes want to share it with certain people. We could do that manually by going to the share settings in the spreadsheet, but a quicker way is to include it in the code, when you are creating the spreadsheet.

```
10.   //Add an editor and viewers to the new spreadsheet
11.   function example2() {
12.     const originalSs =
        SpreadsheetApp.openById('1ZI_sgQ3SGbVs4WZwYt6kuMszYFHsngLvtVbnXvvZIwQ'),
13.     ss2 = originalSs.copy("NEW"); //Normally don't include this line
14.     ss2.rename("example2");
15.     ss2.addEditor('brgablog2@gmail.com');
16.     ss2.addViewers(['brgablogse@gmail.com', 'brgablogesp@gmail.com']);
17.   }
```

Line 11: Set up function *example2*.

Line 12: Let's make a copy of an existing spreadsheet. First, let's open it by its ID.

Line 13: Here, I'm going to make a copy of it so that it appears in your My Drive. Normally in the code you wouldn't need this step. Let's make a copy and temporarily call it "NEW". I've added it so it will appear in your My Drive.

Line 14: Here, I'm going to rename it "example2" using the **rename()** method. Obviously, normally you wouldn't copy a spreadsheet and give it a name then rename it straight afterwards, but I wanted to show the **rename()** method.

Line 15: Now, we're going to add another editor. This is simply done by using **addEditor()** and in the brackets adding their email address between quote marks.

Line 16: Similarly, we can add viewers (i.e. those without edit rights). Here, we're going to add more than one person at the same time, so we use the plural viewer<u>s</u> not viewer and we need to add the email addresses as an array. So, as you can see, in the brackets we add square brackets and list the email addresses with a comma between them.

Note, **addEditors()** also exists as does **addViewer()**.

Run the code, and you'll see the new spreadsheet in your My Drive. As you can see by the people symbol to the right of the name, it has been shared.

 example2

Click on the sharing icon at the top of the screen.

You'll see that we have indeed given edit rights to one user and view access to two other users.

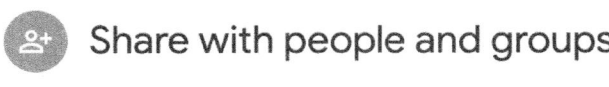

B	**Barrie Roberts (you)** bazrobertsbooks@gmail.com	Owner
I	**Ian Student** brgablog2@gmail.com	Editor ▼
R	**Roberto Barri** brgablogesp@gmail.com	Viewer ▼
S	**Student Example** brgablogse@gmail.com	Viewer ▼

Example 3 – Moving a sheet to a new location

This time, let's get the sheet called "All", which is currently the second sheet in the spreadsheet and move it to the last sheet position on the right.

Sheet1 ▼   All ▼   Unique Methods ▼   SS Methods ▼   Sheet Methods ▼

```
19.  //Move a specific sheet to a new location
20.  function example3() {
21.    const currentSs = SpreadsheetApp.getActiveSpreadsheet(),
22.      ss3 = currentSs.copy("example3"),
23.      sheetAll = ss3.getSheetByName("All");
24.    sheetAll.activate();
25.    ss3.moveActiveSheet(5);
26.  }
```

Line 21: Get the active spreadsheet and store it in *currentSs*.

Line 22: Let's make a copy of it, so you have a copy in your My Drive, and let's call it "example3". We store the new spreadsheet in *ss3*.

Line 23: Now, let's get the sheet we want by using **getSheetByName()**. So, we use this with the spreadsheet *ss3* and add the name of the sheet in the brackets between quote marks.

Line 24: As we're going to use the **moveActiveSheet()** method to move the sheet, we first need to activate this sheet. So, we use the variable *sheetAll* and use the **activate()** method.

Line 25: Finally, we get the spreadsheet *ss3*, use **moveActiveSheet()** and state which position we want the sheet to move to. As here it will be at the end and there are 5 sheets, we need to put 5.

Run the code and you'll see the new spreadsheet in your My Drive.

example3

Open it and you'll see the sheet called "All" has been moved to the last position to the right.

Sheet1 ▼   Unique Methods ▼   SS Methods ▼   Sheet Methods ▼   All ▼

To move it to the front we would put 1.

Example 4 – Moving a sheet to a new location using getNumSheets()

Sometimes, we don't know how many sheets they are in our spreadsheet beforehand or maybe there are a lot to count, so instead of stating a fixed number upfront, we can get the code to count the number of sheets and then place the sheet where we want in relation to that number. Here, we're going to move the "All" sheet again to the end.

```
28.    //Move a sheet to a new location using getNumSheets
29.    function example4() {
30.      const currentSs = SpreadsheetApp.getActiveSpreadsheet(),
31.          ss4 = currentSs.copy("example4"),
32.          sheetAll = ss4.getSheetByName("All");
33.      sheetAll.activate();
34.      const numOfSheets = ss4.getNumSheets();
35.      ss4.moveActiveSheet(numOfSheets);
36.    }
```

Lines 29-33: As before, we get the active spreadsheet, make a copy, get the sheet "All" and activate it.

Line 34: This time, let's get the total number of sheets in our new spreadsheet. We use **getNumSheets()** and we'll store the number in the variable *numOfSheets*.

Line 35: Now, let's move that sheet to the number in *numOfSheets*, i.e. 5, as there are 5 sheets.

Run the code, and you'll see the new spreadsheet in your My Drive. As before, we can see that the "All" sheet is in the last position.

example4

Sheet1 ▼ | Unique Methods ▼ | SS Methods ▼ | Sheet Methods ▼ | All ▼

This is a useful method, not only to position the sheet at the end but to move it to other positions in relation to the end. For example, we could position it in the penultimate position, just by subtracting one from the number of sheets, i.e. (*numOfSheets*-1).

Example 5 – Inserting and deleting sheets

In this final example, we're going to insert a sheet at the end and delete the first sheet in a spreadsheet. We're also going to see how we can get a sheet by its position, not just by its name.

```
38.  //Insert a new sheet and delete a sheet
39.  function example5() {
40.    const currentSs = SpreadsheetApp.getActiveSpreadsheet(),
41.      ss5 = currentSs.copy("example5"),
42.      numOfSheets = ss5.getNumSheets();
43.    ss5.insertSheet(numOfSheets);
44.    const firstSheet = ss5.getSheets()[0];
45.    ss5.deleteSheet(firstSheet);
46.  }
```

Lines 39-41: We get the active spreadsheet and make a copy.

Line 42: Let's get the total number of sheets in our spreadsheet, using **getNumSheets()** and store the number in *numOfSheets*.

Line 43: Let's insert a sheet at the end. To do so, we use the **insertSheet()** method and then add *numOfSheets* in the brackets.

Line 44: To delete the first sheet, first we need to get the sheet. Here, we're going to get the sheet by using its position. We get the spreadsheet and then use **getSheets()** and in square brackets put the position we want, so in this case, 0. It's 0 as we're using an array. **getSheets()** actually gets all the sheets in the spreadsheet and stores them in an array, which we can access just by stating the array position.

Line 45: Now, we can delete that sheet by using **deleteSheet()**.

As we can see, it's created the spreadsheet and in the spreadsheet, it's inserted a new sheet called "Sheet2" and deleted the sheet called "Sheet1".

example5

All ▾   Unique Methods ▾   SS Methods ▾   Sheet Methods ▾   Sheet2 ▾

You can see how easy it is to use the Spreadsheet class to copy and name spreadsheets, and move sheets.

Find more information on the **Spreadsheet** class here:

https://developers.google.com/apps-script/reference/spreadsheet/spreadsheet

You can find the full piece of code for this chapter in Appendix 1.

CHAPTER 8 – Sheet Class

In the previous chapters, we've looked at the **SpreadsheetApp** and **Spreadsheet** classes. Now, let's look at the next level down, which is the **Sheet** class.

Class Sheet   Send feedback

Access and modify spreadsheet sheets. Common operations are renaming a sheet and accessing range objects from the sheet.

https://developers.google.com/apps-script/reference/spreadsheet/sheet

Here, we'll look at how we can work with sheets in a spreadsheet, and in particular, I'll highlight the following common tasks:

- Copying and renaming a master sheet
- Adding data from one sheet to another
- Hiding, inserting, and deleting rows and columns in a sheet
- Appending data to a list and then sorting that list
- Automatically adjusting the column width
- Getting a row of data from a full list, creating a new sheet and adding the individual's info
- Speeding up writing to a sheet by using arrays

In the examples below, we'll be using a file which has 4 sheets: *name*, *teachers*, *classes*, and a hidden one called *master*.

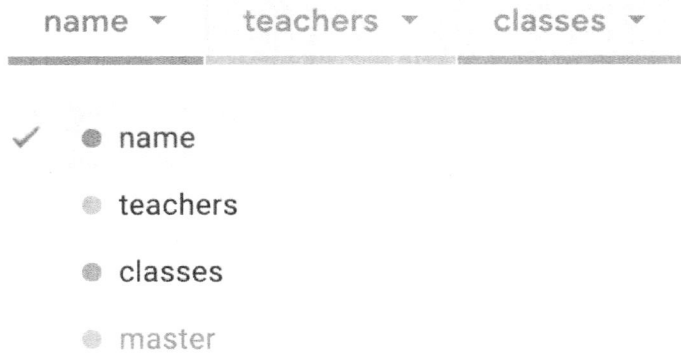

104

Example 1 – Copying a hidden master sheet and renaming it

Here, we're going to make a copy of a master sheet (below) for a teacher to fill out, rename it with the teacher's name, which is on the sheet called *"name"*, and add their name to a cell on the newly created sheet.

	A	B	C	D	E	F
1						
2	Classes	Timetables	Num of students	Classroom	Start date	Finish date
3						
4						
5						
6						
7						
8						

```
1. //Makes a copy of a hidden master sheet and renames it with the teacher's
   name
2. function example1() {
3.    const ss = SpreadsheetApp.getActiveSpreadsheet(),
4.          ssId = ss.getId(),
5.          destination = SpreadsheetApp.openById(ssId),
6.          master = ss.getSheetByName("master"),
7.          newSheet = master.copyTo(destination);
```

Line 2: Set up the function and we'll call it *example1*.

Line 3: Get the active spreadsheet and store it in the variable *ss*.

Line 4: To tell the code where to put the new sheet, we need the spreadsheet ID. As we're going to copy the sheet to the same spreadsheet, we just get the active spreadsheet, *ss*, and get its ID.

Line 5: Getting its ID isn't enough, we also need to open it by its ID. Let's store that in the variable *destination*. Note, this doesn't open it in your browser, it 'opens' it on the server side allowing you to work with it.

Line 6: Now, let's get the master sheet we want to copy, by getting it by its name.

Line 7: To copy a sheet, we use the **copyTo()** method. This can copy a sheet to another spreadsheet or in this case, to the same spreadsheet. We get the master sheet and copy it to the same opened spreadsheet.

```
9.      newSheet.showSheet();
10.     const teachersName = ss.getSheetByName("name").getRange("A1").getValue();
11.     newSheet.setName(teachersName);
12.     newSheet.getRange("A1").setValue(teachersName);
13.   }
```

Line 9: As the master sheet in this spreadsheet is hidden, we need to show the newly created sheet. By default, the copied sheet will be hidden if the sheet its being copied from is hidden. The master sheet doesn't have to be hidden, but I often hide sheets that are not in use for the user. To do this, we use **showSheet()**.

Line 10: The teacher's name we want to name the sheet is on the sheet called "name" in cell A1. So, we get the sheet by its name, get the cell A1 and its value.

	A
1	Barrie Harris-Roberts

Line 11: Then, we rename the sheet with the **setName()** method.

Line 12: I also want to add the teacher's name on the new sheet, so we get cell A1 and set its value to the teacher's name.

Run the code, then open the spreadsheet and you'll see the new sheet with the teacher's name.

Barrie Harris-Roberts ▼

Open the sheet and you'll see it's copied the master sheet and added the teacher's name. Note, that by using the **copyTo** it doesn't copy over the cell's background colour. This could be added by getting the range and using **setBackground()**.

	A	B	C	D	E	F
1	**Barrie Harris-Roberts**					
2	Classes	Timetables	Num of students	Classroom	Start date	Finish date
3						
4						
5						
6						
7						
8						

Example 2 – Hiding and inserting rows and columns

Here, we're going to use the list of classes on the classes sheet and hide some rows and columns to display only certain information.

	A	B	C	D	E	F	G
1	Teachers	Classes	Timetables	Num of students	Classroom	Start date	Finish date
2	Wilma McCartney	A1	09:00-11:00	8	A01	01/10/2017	30/06/2018
3	Fred Lennon	B2	10:00-12:00	12	A02	01/10/2017	20/12/2017
4	Barney Starr	C1	17:00-20:00	10	A03	05/10/2017	30/06/2018
5	Betty Harrison	C2	09:30-11:00	12	A04	13/10/2017	20/12/2017

We're just going to leave the list of teachers, the timetables, the number of students and we're going to insert an extra column, so that the user can add some notes to the rows.

	A	C	D	E
2	Wilma McCartney	09:00-11:00	8	
3	Fred Lennon	10:00-12:00	12	
4	Barney Starr	17:00-20:00	10	
5	Betty Harrison	09:30-11:00	12	

```
15. //Hides certain columns and the header row, and inserts a blank column
16. //Then deletes all the blank rows and columns
17. function example2() {
18.   const ss = SpreadsheetApp.getActiveSpreadsheet(),
19.         classes = ss.getSheetByName("classes");
20.   classes.hideColumns(2);
21.   classes.hideColumns(5, 3);
22.   classes.hideRows(1);
23.   classes.insertColumns(5);
```

Lines 17-18: We set up the function and get the active spreadsheet.

Line 19: We then get the sheet called "classes" and store it in the variable *classes*.

Line 20: To hide columns we use the **hideColumns()** method and in the brackets we state which column we want to hide. In this case, it's column B (the second column).

Line 21: I also want to hide the columns E to G. Fortunately, we can hide a range of columns in one go. We use the same **hideColumns()** method, but this time we include 2 arguments, firstly the position of the first column we want to hide, in this case column 5 (column E). Then, we state how many columns we want to hide, so, in this case 3.

Line 22: We can hide rows in a similar way, this time using **hideRows()**. Here, I'm hiding the header row.

Line 23: I want to insert a column next to the student numbers in position 5. To do so, we use **insertColumns()** and add the column position number.

```
25.     const lastRow = classes.getLastRow(),
26.           maxRow = classes.getMaxRows(),
27.           blankRows = maxRow - lastRow;
28.     if(blankRows > 0){
29.       classes.deleteRows(lastRow + 1, blankRows);
30.     }
```

Now, I want to delete all the blank rows below the table. To do so, we need to find out which is the last row with values in it and which is the last row on the sheet.

Line 25: First, let's find out the last row with information on it. We use **getLastRow()** to do this. This will return the row number, in this case, 5, and we'll store it in the variable *lastRow*.

Line 26: Next, we get the last row on the sheet (with or without data in it). We use **getMaxRows()** to do this. Again, this returns the row number, in this case, it's 1,000 and store it in the variable *maxRow*.

Line 27: Now, we use these two figures to work out how many rows to delete. We subtract *lastRow* from *maxRow* and store it in the variable *blankRows*.

Now, we can delete the rows, but only want to do it if there are rows to delete. If there are no blank rows below the table, *blankRows* will be 0, and there is no need to delete anything.

Line 28: So, first we check if *blankRows* is bigger than 0, i.e. there are rows to delete.

Line 29: To delete rows we use **deleteRows()**. There are 2 arguments, the first, which row we will start from, and the second is how many rows. So, we want to start from the row below the last row with text, so *lastRow* + 1. Then, the number of rows is the figure we calculated before, which is in *blankRows*.

Note, if we didn't have the conditional there, and we tried to delete 0 rows, it would throw an error.

```
32.     const lastColumn = classes.getLastColumn(),
33.           maxColumn = classes.getMaxColumns(),
34.           blankColumns = maxColumn - lastColumn;
35.     if(blankColumns > 0){
36.       classes.deleteColumns(lastColumn + 1, blankColumns);
37.     }
38. }
```

I also want to delete the blank columns to the right of the table. This is done in a similar way as deleting the rows, but of course, this time we're working with columns not rows.

Run the *example2* function and you'll be left with this:

	A	C	D	E
2	Wilma McCartney	09:00-11:00	8	
3	Fred Lennon	10:00-12:00	12	
4	Barney Starr	17:00-20:00	10	
5	Betty Harrison	09:30-11:00	12	

If you run *example2*, you will have to manually reset the sheet, if you want to run it again. Otherwise, you'll get a different result the second time as a column has been inserted and has changed the position of the columns to the right of it.

This is useful if you regularly print certain parts of the sheet, so you can run a quick bit of code to set the sheet up the way you want, print the sheet, then run another piece of code that resets the sheet. This saves you having to do it manually every time.

Example 3 – Appending a name to a list and sorting it alphabetically

This time, we're going to get a teacher's name from the "name" sheet and add it to the list of teachers on the "teachers" sheet. Then, we're going to sort that list alphabetically and also, adjust the column width automatically, so that the names fit in the cells.

This could be useful for example, if the name has been received from a form submission and then you're adding that name to some kind of master list. To keep the code simple, we're just going to get it from a specific cell, which is cell A1 on the "names" sheet.

	A
1	Barrie Harris-Roberts

Here's the current list on the "teachers" sheet.

	A
1	Barney Starr
2	Betty Harrison
3	Fred Lennon
4	Wilma McCartney

```
40.  //Adds teachers name to a list of teachers on a different sheet
41.  //Then adjusts the column width automatically and sorts the list
42.  function example3() {
43.    const ss = SpreadsheetApp.getActiveSpreadsheet(),
44.          teachersName = ss.getSheetByName("name").getRange("A1").getValue(),
45.          teachersList = ss.getSheetByName("teachers");
46.    teachersList.appendRow([teachersName]);
```

Lines 42-43: Set up the function and get the active spreadsheet.

Line 44: Let's get the name we want from the name sheet in cell A1.

Line 45: Now, let's get the sheet we want to edit, which is the "teachers" sheet.

Line 46: To add the name at the bottom of the list, we use the **appendRow()** method, which will automatically work out where the bottom of the list is and add the name under it. Note that, it expects an array here, so, the teacher's name needs to be in the square brackets.

The Google documentation for **appendRow()** shows want parameter type is required:

Name	Type	Description
rowContents	Object[]	An array of values to insert after the last row in the sheet.

As you can see, it states "Object[]" and in the description states it's an array it needs.

```
48.    teachersList.autoResizeColumn(1);
49.    teachersList.sort(1);
50.  }
```

Line 48: Now, let's adjust the column width so that all the names fit within the cells. We do this with **autoResizeColumn()** and state which column on the sheet we want to adjust, which in this case is column 1 (column A).

Line 49: Finally, let's sort our list alphabetically. We do this with the **sort()** method and in the brackets state which column will be sorted.

Note, if you have other columns with data that's connected to the column you want to sort, they won't be changed, so, this could mess up your data. So, only use this sheet sorting for individual columns. In the next chapter, we'll look at sorting data with multiple columns.

Run the *example3* function and as you will see, it's added the new teacher's name, sorted the list and made the column width wider to accommodate the longest teacher's name.

	A
1	Barney Starr
2	Barrie Harris-Roberts
3	Betty Harrison
4	Fred Lennon
5	Wilma McCartney

Example 4 – Extracting data from a table and creating a new sheet with that data

Here, we're going to extract a particular teacher's data, insert a new sheet, and add that teacher's data to the new sheet.

	A	B	C	D	E	F	G
1	Teachers	Classes	Timetables	Num of students	Classroom	Start date	Finish date
2	Wilma McCartney	A1	09:00-11:00	8	A01	01/10/2017	30/06/2018
3	Fred Lennon	B2	10:00-12:00	12	A02	01/10/2017	20/12/2017
4	Barney Starr	C1	17:00-20:00	10	A03	05/10/2017	30/06/2018
5	Betty Harrison	C2	09:30-11:00	12	A04	13/10/2017	20/12/2017

```
52.    //Asks the user for the teacher's row number then makes a new sheet for
       that teacher with their class details
53.    function example4(){
54.      const ui = SpreadsheetApp.getUi(),
55.            response = ui.prompt('Teacher', 'Which teacher do you want?
       Enter row number.', ui.ButtonSet.OK_CANCEL);
56.      if (response.getSelectedButton() === ui.Button.OK) {
57.        const rowNumber = response.getResponseText();
58.      }
```

Firstly, we're going to ask for the row number corresponding to the teacher we want. I've done this just to keep the code simple and also the user will only have to type in a number, rather than a full name. Lines 54-58 prompt the user to enter a row number and that response is then stored.

Line 54: Access the spreadsheet user-interface with **SpreadsheetApp.getUi()**.

Line 55: Display the prompt dialogue box, using **prompt()**. In the brackets, state the title of the prompt, the question you want to ask, and the buttons you want to show, in this case, there will be an OK and Cancel button.

Line 56: Then, we need to get the response if they clicked the OK button. Here, we get the selected button and if it equals the OK button then it will run line 57. If cancel button is clicked, the prompt box closes and nothing happens.

Line 57: We get the text of the response by using **getResponseText()** and store it in the *rowNumber* variable.

Line 58: Close the **if** statement.

```
60.    const ss = SpreadsheetApp.getActiveSpreadsheet(),
61.          classes = ss.getSheetByName("classes"),
62.          teachers = classes.getDataRange().getValues();
```

Line 60: Get the active spreadsheet.

Line 61: Get the sheet called "classes".

Line 62: Get all the values on that sheet by using the **getDataRange()** method and store them in the variable *teachers*.

```
64.     const teachersName = teachers[rowNumber - 1][0],
65.           newSheet = ss.insertSheet(teachersName);
```

Line 64: Now, we just want the specific teacher's row. We do that by getting a specific 'row' and 'column' within our array *teachers*. The first number in the square brackets is the row number, where we will use the variable *rowNumber* we got from the prompt before. As this is an array we have to minus 1, as for example, row 1 is in position 0 in the array. The second number is the column number, again this is zero-based, so the first column is in position 0.

Line 65: Now, we need to insert the new sheet We do this by using the **insertSheet()** method and add the name of the sheet in the brackets.

```
67.     const headers = teachers.shift(),
68.           teacherInfo = teachers[rowNumber - 2];
```

I want to get the headers and then the teacher's row.

Line 67: To get the header row, we can use the **shift()** method with our array. This will extract the data in the first position of our array and we'll then store it in the *headers* variable. I.e. it will extract just the header row in our table.

Here's the content of *headers*:

[Teachers, Classes, Timetables, Num of students, Classrocm, Start date, Finish date]

As **shift()** has removed the headers data from the array, the data in row 2 is now in position 0 in our array.

We can see the content of *teachers* now the first row has been removed:

[[Wilma McCartney, A1, 09:00-11:00, 8, A01, 01/10/2017, 30/06/2018], [Fred Lennon, B2, 10:00-12:00, 12, A02, 01/10/2017, 20/12/2017], [Barney Starr, C1, 17:00-20:00, 10, A03, 05/10/2017, 30/06/2018], [Betty Harrison, C2, 09:30-11:00, 12, A04, 13/10/2017, 20/12/2017]]

Line 68: So, to get the teacher's data we need to get the row number and instead of subtracting one for our array, we need to subtract 2. Here, we just use one set of square brackets as we are going to get the data in the whole row, so we don't state which column we want.

```
70.     newSheet.appendRow(headers);
71.     newSheet.appendRow(teacherInfo);
72.   }
```

Now, we need to add the headers row and teacher's information.

Line 70: First, we append the row with the headers to the new sheet.

Line 71: Finally, we append the row with the teacher's info.

Run the function *example4*. Open the spreadsheet and you'll see the prompt box asking you for the row number. Enter the number you want and click OK.

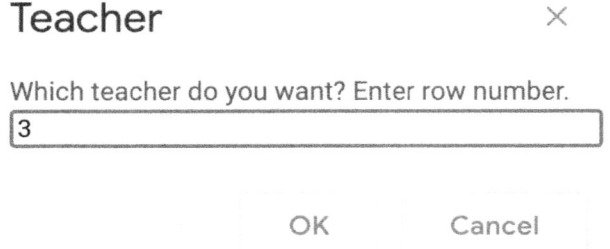

The new sheet will be added with the teacher's name.

Fred Lennon ▾

Open the sheet and you'll see that the headers and teacher's information has been added. Note, this is unformatted as we only got the values from the original sheet, but the sheet could easily be formatted.

	A	B	C	D	E	F	G
1	Teachers	Classes	Timetables	Num of students	Classroom	Start date	Finish date
2	Fred Lennon	B2	10:00-12:00	12	A02	01/10/2017	20/12/2017

Example 5 – Extracting data from a table and creating a new sheet with that data (Quicker method)

The above code is fine but here I want to show you why we would avoid making multiple **appendRow** calls. Every time, we interact with the spreadsheet, we are calling for information and that takes an amount of time. What we should try to do in our code, is to get and set the information we want in single calls, to reduce the number of calls and therefore, the time taken.

The code is the same as above until line 90.

```
74.    //The same as example4 but a quicker way
75.    function example5(){
76.      const ui = SpreadsheetApp.getUi(),
77.            response = ui.prompt('Teacher', 'Which teacher do you want? Enter row number.', ui.ButtonSet.OK_CANCEL);
78.      if (response.getSelectedButton() === ui.Button.OK) {
79.        const rowNumber = response.getResponseText();
80.      }

82.      const ss = SpreadsheetApp.getActiveSpreadsheet(),
83.            classes = ss.getSheetByName("classes"),
84.            teachers = classes.getDataRange().getValues();
85.
86.      const teachersName = teachers[rowNumber - 1][0],
87.            newSheet = ss.insertSheet(teachersName);
88.
89.      const headers = teachers.shift(),
90.            teacherInfo = teachers[rowNumber - 2];
91.
92.      const info = [];
93.      info.push(headers);
94.      info.push(teacherInfo);
```

We're going to create an array in which we will add the headers and teacher's information.

Line 92: First, we set up the empty array. We do this by assigning a variable to the empty square brackets.

Note, I said earlier that constants don't change, but that's not completely true. Constants can change in certain circumstances, for example, here we're going to add to the array, and that's possible with **const**, but it still ensures we don't accidently reassign a different value or data type to it.

Line 93: Then, we add the data we want into the array. One way of doing that is to use the **push()** method. So, first we add the headers info, which will be in position 0 of our array.

Line 94: Then, we push the teacher's info, which will be in position 1 (i.e. added to the end of the array).

```
96.    newSheet.getRange(1,1,info.length,info[0].length).setValues(info);
97. }
```

Line 96: In the previous example, we appended each row separately, but here we'll get the range on the new sheet and add the contents of the *info* array in one go.

Note, that we need to get a range that is the same dimensions as our array, *info*, otherwise it'll throw an error. We can do that by getting the length of the *info* array (i.e. how many rows: 2), and the length of the first row (i.e. how many columns: 7). We get how many rows, by getting the length of the array. We get how columns by getting the length of a particular row (usually the first one).

Running the function will produce the same result as before. If you ran the previous example before, make sure you either delete the sheet that was made before running this one, or choose a different teacher this time, otherwise it will try to make a sheet with the same name and this isn't possible, so an error will appear.

The reason I added this last example, was to show you the difference in time taken to complete the same overall task. Unfortunately, in the new script editor, the execution log doesn't show the time for each step in the code and we can't compare the two as a whole as we are using a prompt and of course it will include the time we take to fill in the prompt question with the teacher's row.

However, using the old editor and old version of Apps Script, appending the 2 rows took 0.581 seconds (0.308s + 0.281s), whereas, setting the values in one go, only took 0.12s to complete the same task.

While in this simple example, we're only talking a difference of less than half a second, example 4 was **5 times slower** than example 5. In a larger program, this could mean that either the user has to wait longer for the program to finish or at worst, will mean the program reaches the 6-minute runtime limit and stops working. So, it's important to think of not just how you get something done but the quickest and most efficient way to do it.

This is also why we use **getDataRange()** (e.g. in line 80) to get all the data in one go and store it in an array. We then work with the array, rather than calling for different ranges from our sheet, which would be slower.

If you want to learn more about **push()** and **shift()** methods visit the W3schools site:

https://www.w3schools.com/jsref/jsref_push.asp

https://www.w3schools.com/jsref/jsref_shift.asp

Plus, find more information on the **Sheet** class here:

https://developers.google.com/apps-script/reference/spreadsheet/sheet

You can find the full piece of code for this chapter in Appendix 1.

CHAPTER 9 – Range class & Triggers

So far, we've looked at the classes **SpreadsheetApp**, **Spreadsheet**, and **Sheet**. Now we're getting to the smallest component, the Range. In this chapter, we're going to look at some of the ways you can control the cells on your spreadsheet, using the methods connected to the **Range** class.

At the time of writing, there were nearly 200 different methods connected to this class. So, as you can imagine there are a lot of different things you can do with ranges. Here, I'm going to take you through some examples, showing you some of the common methods used when working with ranges, and if you've already read the previous chapters, it'll give you a chance to consolidate some of the knowledge you now have on the other spreadsheet-related classes.

Class Range

Access and modify spreadsheet ranges. A range can be a single cell in a sheet or a group of adjacent cells in a sheet.

The main areas we're going to look are:

- activating cells and clearing their content
- setting up triggers automatically (onOpen, onEdit, onFormSubmit)
- adding formulas to cells
- changing the number format of cells
- adding borders and changing the alignment
- changing the background colour based on edits to a range
- sorting a table by multiple columns
- copying part of a range and creating a new sheet with that range

So, let's dive into the first example.

Example 1 – On opening a spreadsheet, highlight a specific cell & clear its content

By default, when we open spreadsheets, the first page is shown and cell A1 is highlighted, but there are times when we want to take the user directly to a specific cell, maybe to enter some information. Here, as a simple example, I want the cell B4 to be highlighted ready for the user to type in the name of the book they are looking for in an inventory.

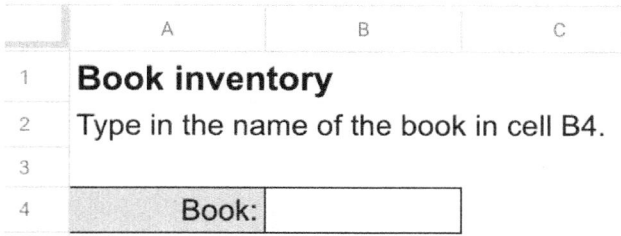

```
1.  //EXAMPLE 1 - Open sheet, highlight a certain cell and clear its content
2.  function onOpen() {
3.    const ss = SpreadsheetApp.getActiveSpreadsheet(),
4.          sheet1 = ss.getSheetByName("eg1"),
5.          cell = sheet1.getRange("B4");
6.    cell.activate()
7.       .clearContent();
8.  }
```

Line 2: First, we set up the **onOpen()** trigger. By calling the function '**onOpen()**', this will run the function automatically when the spreadsheet is opened. As we saw in an earlier chapter, we often use this to create menus, that are added as soon as the spreadsheet is loaded.

Line 3: Let's get the active spreadsheet.

Line 4: This file contains various sheets, so let's get the first one cal ed "*eg1*".

Line 5: Now, I need to get the range I want to highlight, which is B4.

Line 6: To highlight it, we need to activate the cell. So, we use the **activate()** method. We're going to chain another method to this, so don't add a semi-colon on the end.

Line 7: As a previous user might have already typed something in that cell, I also want to remove any content in it, to make it ready for this user. To do so, we use **clearContent()**. This will remove the values in the cell.

There are a few different clear methods, some which clear the format, clear everything, clear notes, etc, but here I just want to clear any text that was left in there.

Open the spreadsheet and you'll see sheet *eg1* will be opened and cell B4 is highlighted.

Notice how we first got the spreadsheet (*ss*), then the sheet (*sheet1*), then the specific range, in this case a cell (*cell*).

Example 2 – Add a formula to a cell when a form is submitted

Here, we're going to add a formula to a sheet when a form connected to it has been submitted. To do this automatically, we need to set up the trigger **onFormSubmit()**. We could do this manually by clicking on the triggers menu (clock icon on the menu on the left-hand side), but here let's set it up programmatically. Below is a function to set up the **onFormSubmit** trigger. You'll need to run it before running the function *example2*.

```
10.  //EXAMPLE 2 - Set up onFormSubmit trigger
11.  function example2Trigger() {
12.    const ss = SpreadsheetApp.getActiveSpreadsheet();
13.    ScriptApp.newTrigger("example2")
14.              .forSpreadsheet(ss)
15.              .onFormSubmit()
16.              .create();
17.  }
```

Line 12: Get the active spreadsheet.

Line 13: We use the **ScriptApp** class to do this, then add the **newTrigger()** method. In the brackets, refer to the function you want to run when the form is submitted. In this case it will be the *example2* function, which I'll explain below. Don't add a semi-colon at the end, as all the following methods are chained together.

Line 14: Next, we need to state where the trigger will come from, and in this case it will be when the form response is submitted and stored in the spreadsheet. We use **forSpreadsheet()** and state the spreadsheet in the brackets, which in this case is the active one we stored earlier in the variable *ss*.

Line 15: Then, we state the trigger type we want. Here it's the **onFormSubmit** one.

Line 16: Finally, we tell it to create the trigger.

Run this function once you've written the function *example2*, otherwise the reference to the function will throw an error.

If we look in the triggers (clicking on the clock icon on the toolbar), we can see it's been set up for us:

Triggers						Showing 1 trigger
+ Add a filter						
Owned by	Last run	Deployment	Event		Function	Error rate
Me	-	Head	From spreadsheet - On form submit		example2	-

Now, in this simple example, the employee will fill in a form with their start and finish time and this will be recorded on the Sheet. We then want to calculate the hours they have worked by adding a formula on the same response row. We're going to work with the sheet called *eg2*, which is where the form has been linked to.

Clocking in and out

*Required

Start time *

Time

:

Finish time *

Time

:

Submit

```
19.  //EXAMPLE 2 - Add formula to last row, which is triggered when a form is
     submitted
20.  function example2() {
21.    const ss = SpreadsheetApp.getActiveSpreadsheet(),
22.          sheet2 = ss.getSheetByName("eg2"),
```

121

```
23.        lastRow = sheet2.getLastRow();
24.     sheet2.getRange(lastRow,4).setFormulaR1C1("=R[0]C[-1]-R[0]C[-2]");
25.  }
```

Line 22: Let's get the sheet where the responses will appear, *eg2*.

Line 23: When a form is submitted, the latest response is appended to the next row that doesn't have any data on it, so is always the last row. We want to get the latest response row, so we use **getLastRow()**.

	A	B	C	D
1	Timestamp	Start time	Finish time	Duration
2	14/03/2021 14:53:10	10:00:00	12:00:00	

Line 24: I want to add the formula for the hours worked in column D. So, first we get the last row and column 4 (column D). Then, using the **setFormulaR1C1()** method we add the formula. We use the R1C1 version as the formula will refer to cells in relation to the formula cell. The formula we want is the cell in column C minus the cell in column B (e.g. C2-B2).

Obviously, as more responses are submitted, the row number will change every time. In the brackets, we write the formula in relation to the formula cell. So, it's row 0 (the same row) one column to the left (-1), minus row 0 two columns to the left (-2). Remember to add the equals sign and surround all the formula in quote marks.

Submitting a form, we can see the start time and finish time have been recorded and the time worked has been added into column D.

	A	B	C	D
1	Timestamp	Start time	Finish time	Duration
2	18/06/2017 14:53:10	10:00:00	12:00:00	02:00:00

Clicking on cell D2, we can see it's added the correct formula:

=C2-B2

Example 3 – Add a formula when a form is submitted and format the responses

This example is similar to example 2, but this time we're going to add a little bit of formatting to our responses as they are submitted. We're going to change the time format, centre the data and add borders to the data.

	A	B	C	D
1	Timestamp	Start time	Finish time	Duration
2	18/06/2017	09:00	12:00	03:00
3	18/06/2017	10:00	12:30	02:30

First, we create a trigger as before, this time referring it to function *example3*.

```
27. //EXAMPLE 3 - Set up onFormSubmit trigger
28. function example3Trigger() {
29.   const ss = SpreadsheetApp.getActiveSpreadsheet();
30.   ScriptApp.newTrigger("example3")
31.            .forSpreadsheet(ss)
32.            .onFormSubmit()
33.            .create();
34. }
```

The form is similar to before and I've linked it to sheet *eg3* on the spreadsheet.

Clocking in and out

*Required

Start time *

Time

:

Finish time *

Time

:

Submit

```
36.   //EXAMPLE 3 - Add formula, add formatting when a form is submitted
37.   function example3() {
38.     const ss = SpreadsheetApp.getActiveSpreadsheet(),
39.           sheet3 = ss.getSheetByName("eg3"),
40.           lastRow = sheet3.getLastRow();
41.
42.     sheet3.getRange(lastRow,4).setFormulaR1C1("=R[0]C[-1]-R[0]C[-2]");
```

Lines 37-42: These are the same as described above.

```
44.     const times = sheet3.getRange(lastRow,2,1,3);
45.     times.setNumberFormat("HH:mm");
```

Now, let's add some formatting. First, let's change the times in columns B to D to only show the hours and minutes.

Line 44: First, we get the range of cells using **getRange()** and in the brackets including 4 parameters: starting row number, starting column number, number of rows, number of columns. So, we're getting the last row, column 2, only 1 row, and 3 columns in total. I've stored that range in the variable *times*.

Line 45: Then, we use the **setNumberFormat()** method to state the format we want, which we add in the brackets.

```
47.    const data = sheet3.getDataRange();
48.    data.setHorizontalAlignment("center")
49.       .setBorder(true, true, true, true, true, true);
```

Now, to centre all the data and add borders. To make it simple, I'm just going to get all the data on the sheet and apply the same formatting, not just the latest row.

Line 47: Get all the data on the sheet by using **getDataRange()**.

Line 48: To this range, I'll first centre the text, by setting the horizontal alignment to 'center'.

Line 49: To the same range, I want to add borders. use the method **setBorder()** and this takes 6 parameters, depending on which border you want to add. Here we're adding them to all the sides, so we add the boolean 'true' to all 6 parameters.

```
51.    sheet3.getRange(lastRow,1).setNumberFormat("DD/MM/YYYY");
52. }
```

Line 51: Finally, let's change the timestamp to just show the date. Again, we use **setNumberFormat()** just with a different format in the brackets.

Submit a form and we can see it then formats the cells the way we wanted them.

	A	B	C	D
1	Timestamp	Start time	Finish time	Duration
2	18/06/2017	09:00	12:00	03:00
3	18/06/2017	10:00	12:30	02:30

Example 4 – Change cell colour when a specific cell is edited, using onEdit()

In this example, we're going to use a different trigger called **onEdit()**. This 'listens' for any edits on the spreadsheet and will carry out any actions linked to that event. One of the mistakes sometimes people make when using **onEdit()** is leaving it open so that it reacts to anything edited on your spreadsheet, which is often not what you want. Normally, you want to react to something happening in a specific range of cells.

So, in the simple example below, we have an action plan and when the action status is changed to 'Open' it highlights the cell background in red, and when it's changed to 'Closed' it changes it to green.

	A	B	C
1	**Problem**	**Action**	**Status**
2	Chair broken.	New chair bought.	Closed
3	Whiteboard not turning on.	New batteries fitted.	Closed
4	No Internet.		Open
5	Videos not playing.		

```
57.  function onEdit(e) {
58.    const sh = SpreadsheetApp.getActiveSheet(),
59.          status = e.value,
60.          range = e.range,
61.          column = range.getColumn(),
62.          row = range.getRow();
```

Line 57: We call the function **onEdit()** to set up the **onEdit** trigger. To capture the event, we need to add a parameter in the brackets, so we can use it later on. Here, I've used "e" for event, which is common to see in programs.

Line 58: Get the active sheet.

Now we need to get the range stored in the event and its value. Here's what the event contains:

`{user=, source=Spreadsheet, oldValue=Closed, authMode=LIMITED, range=Range, value=Open}`

The information is stored as **objects** with the **property** of the object assigned to it. For example, we can see that the value is Open and the old value was Closed. To get the property, we need to get the event and then the object. We do this by joining the two together with a dot. For example, to get the value in the cell, we use **e.value**.

Line 59: We then need to find out what value was entered on the cell that was edited. We get the value of the event.

Line 60: Here, we want to find out where that edit happened, So, we get the range of the event, i.e what cell was edited.

Lines 61-62: I also want to find out the row number and column number of that range, so we use **getRow()** and **getColumn()** on that range.

	A	B	C
1	**Problem**	**Action**	**Status**
2	Chair broken.	New chair bought.	Closed
3	Whiteboard not turning on.	New batteries fitted.	Closed
4	No Internet.		Open
5	Videos not playing.		

```
64.    if (sh.getName() === "eg4" && column === 3 && row > 1 && row < 6) {
65.       if(status === "Closed"){
66.          range.setBackground("#66BB6A");
67.       }
```

Now, this is where we will react to the edit only if it is within a certain sheet and range and if it does we'll change the background colour of the cell.

Line 64: First, we want to check that 3 things are true. 1) The edited sheet is called "eg4"; 2) The column number is column 3; 3) The row number is between row 2 and 5. We use an **if** statement to check that and notice we've used the double ampersands (&&) to check that all these conditions are true.

Line 65: If it is, then we check if the status is "Closed".

Line 66: If they are all true, it will get the range and set the background to green. In the brackets here, I've used a hexadecimal colour reference in quote marks.

```
68.       else if(status === "Open"){
69.          range.setBackground("#EF5350");
70.       }
71.    }
72. }
```

Lines 68-72: If the previous if statement was false, then we check if the text states "Open". If it does, we set the background colour to red. If this if statement returns false, then it doesn't do anything.

To try it out, click on one of the cells in column C and change the status to either Open or Closed. The cell background will change to red or green. Note, I've used data validation in column C to show the Open and Closed options as a drop-down menu.

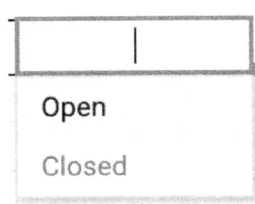

	A	B	C
1	**Problem**	**Action**	**Status**
2	Chair broken.	New chair bought.	Closed
3	Whiteboard not turning on.	New batteries fitted.	Closed
4	No Internet.		Open
5	Videos not playing.		

We could of course just use conditional formatting to do the same thing, but we're here to learn Apps Script right?

Important: If you're using the code that's in the file, you will need to comment out lines 73 to 99, as there is an onEdit trigger in the example below, and you would normally have one in a script file, otherwise it will get confused. To comment it out, just wrote /* in line 73 and */ in line 99.

Example 5 – Highlight whole row when a cell is edited

To take the previous example a step further, let's highlight the whole row red or green, when the user changes the status to Open or Closed.

	A	B	C
1	**Problem**	**Action**	**Status**
2	Chair broken.	New chair bought.	Closed
3	Whiteboard not turning on.	New batteries fitted.	Closed
4	No Internet.		Open
5	Videos not playing.		

```
74.   //EXAMPLE5 - Change row to red or green depending on status
75.   function onEdit(e) {
76.     const sh = SpreadsheetApp.getActiveSheet(),
77.           status = e.value,
78.           range = e.range,
79.           column = range.getColumn(),
```

```
80.        row = range.getRow();
```

Lines 75-80: These are the same as the example above.

```
82.        if(sh.getName() === "eg5" && column === 3 && row > 1 && row < 6){
83.           if(status === "Closed"){
84.              const rowToColor = range.offset(0, -2, 1, 3);
85.              rowToColor.setBackground("#66BB6A");
86.           }
```

Line 82: The only change I've made here is change the sheet name to *eg5*.

Line 83: Then we check if the status is "Closed".

Line 84: This time we want to highlight the row (A to C), so we need to get the range of the edited cell, then select the other cells in that row. We can do that by using **offset()**, which takes the original range and selects another range based on its relationship with the original one.

We're going to use the one with 4 parameters: how many rows we are away from the original one; how many columns away; the number of rows we want; the number of columns we want.

So, let's go through our example here. We want the same row, so we state 0 rows away. We want to start from column A, which is 2 columns to the left of the edited column C, so we state -2 (minus numbers move to the left, positive ones to the right). We only want 1 row, so we state 1. Finally, we want 3 columns (A, B, C), so we state 3 in the last parameter.

Line 85: Then we add the green formatting as before, only this will now set the background of the cells in columns A to C.

```
88.        else if(status === "Open"){
89.           var rowToColor = range.offset(0, -2, 1, 3);
90.           rowToColor.setBackground("#EF5350");
91.        }
```

Lines 88-91: We repeat the same but for the Open status and red formatting.

In the previous example, there was a limitation. If we deleted the Open or Closed status from the cell, the cell wouldn't change back to white again. So, let's add that here.

```
93.        else{
94.           var rowToColor = range.offset(0, -2, 1, 3);
95.           rowToColor.setBackground("#FFFFFF");
96.        }
```

```
97.    }
98.  }
```

Line 93: Here, I've added an extra else if statement that will capture any other change to that column.

Line 94: We highlight the range as before.

Line 95: We then set the background colour to white.

Opening the sheet *eg5*, we can see that the formatting changes for the row as we change the status.

	A	B	C
1	Problem	Action	Status
2	Chair broken.	New chair bought.	Closed
3	Whiteboard not turning on.	New batteries fitted.	Closed
4	No Internet.		Open
5	Videos not playing.		

As mentioned in the previous example, to make this run properly, make sure you only have one onEdit trigger visible in the script. To make this run, you will need to comment out lines 53 to 73.

Example 6 – Sort table by multiple columns

Here, we're going to look at sorting a table of information by more than one column. In the chapter on the Sheet class we saw that we could sort data by one column, but by sorting a specific range we have much more control and we can sort multiple columns in different ways. Here, we have a table showing the exam results of some students. We're going to sort it by their average mark and then by their name.

	A	B	C	D
1	Students	Exam 1	Exam 2	Average
2	Wilma Stone	80%	60%	70%
3	Barney Gravel	80%	80%	80%
4	Fred Pebble	70%	90%	80%
5	Betty Rock	90%	70%	80%

```
100. //EXAMPLE 6 - Sort table by average mark and then by student's name
101. function example6() {
102.   const ss = SpreadsheetApp.getActiveSpreadsheet(),
```

```
103.          sheet6 = ss.getSheetByName("eg6"),
104.          range = sheet6.getDataRange();
105.  range.sort([{column: 4, ascending: false}, {column: 1, ascending: true}]);
106. }
```

Line 103: Get sheet eg6.

Line 104: We get the range of the data on our sheet.

Line 105: We use the **sort()** method to sort our data, then we add the details of the columns we want to sort. Note, the use of the brackets, square brackets (it's an array) and the curly brackets (we're defining certain parameters). The information is written in pairs, the column number and then whether the sort will be in ascending order. If it's descending, then you write false. So, here we're sorting column 4 (the average marks) in descending order (i.e. the highest at the top), and then alphabetically by their names.

Running the code, we can see that it has sorted the list by average mark and as there are 3 students with 80%, we can also see it's sorted them alphabetically by name.

	A	B	C	D
1	Students	Exam 1	Exam 2	Average
2	Barney Gravel	80%	80%	80%
3	Betty Rock	90%	70%	80%
4	Fred Pebble	70%	90%	80%
5	Wilma Stone	80%	60%	70%

Example 7 – Copy part of a table to a new sheet

In this final example, we're going to see how easy it is to copy specific information from one sheet to another. Then, we'll add some formatting on the new sheet.

We'll also see how we can check to see if a sheet with the new sheet's name already exists, and if it does we will delete it, as we can't have 2 sheets with the same name in the spreadsheet.

Here, we're going to copy some rows containing information about the available methods to the Range class.

	A	B	C
1	METHOD	RETURN TYPE	DETAILS
2	activate()	Range	Make this range the active range.
3	breakApart()	Range	Break any multi-column cells in the range into individual cells again.
4	canEdit()	Boolean	Determines whether the user has permission to edit every cell in the range.
5	clear()	Range	Clears the range of contents, formats, and data-validation rules.
6	clear(options)	Range	Clears the range of contents, format, data-validation rules, and/or comments, as specified with the given advanced options.
7	clearContent()	Range	Clears the content of the range, leaving the formatting intact.
8	clearDataValidations()	Range	Clears the data-validation rules for the range.
9	clearFormat()	Range	Clears formatting for this range.
10	clearNote()	Range	Clears the note in the given cell or cells.
11	copyFormatToRange(gridId,column, columnEnd, row,rowEnd)	void	Copy the formatting of the range to the given location.
12	copyFormatToRange(sheet,column, columnEnd, row,rowEnd)	void	Copy the formatting of the range to the given location.
13	copyTo(destination)	void	Copies the data from a range of cells to another range of cells.
14	copyTo(destination, options)	void	Copies the data from a range of cells to another range of cells.
15	copyValuesToRange(gridId,column, columnEnd, row,rowEnd)	void	Copy the content of the range to the given location.
16	copyValuesToRange(sheet,column, columnEnd, row,rowEnd)	void	Copy the content of the range to the given location.
17	getA1Notation()	String	Returns a string description of the range, in A1 notation.
18	getBackground()	String	Returns the background color of the top-left cell in the range (i.e., '#ffffff').
19	getBackgrounds()	String[][]	Returns the background colors of the cells in the range (i.e., '#ffffff').
20	getCell(row, column)	Range	Returns a given cell within a range.
21	getColumn()	Integer	Returns the starting column position for this range.

```
108. //EXAMPLE 7 - Copy part of a table to a new sheet
109. function example7() {
110.   const ss = SpreadsheetApp.getActiveSpreadsheet(),
111.         sheet7 = ss.getSheetByName("eg7"),
112.         range = sheet7.getRange(1, 1, 13, 3);
```

Line 111: Get sheet *eg7*.

Line 112: Let's get the part that has been coloured, so the first 13 rows. So, we use **getRange()** and state we that we want rows 1 to 13 and columns 1 to 3.

```
114.   const checkNewSheet = ss.getSheetByName("new");
115.   if (checkNewSheet) {
116.     ss.deleteSheet(checkNewSheet);
117.   }
```

Now, we need to check that the sheet doesn't already exist. This is particularly important in this example, and you wouldn't be able to run this example more than once without it.

Line 114: First, we get the sheet by its name. The sheet we're going to create will be called "new".

Line 115: Then, we check if there is a sheet called "new". We do this just by using the **if** statement and passing the name of the sheet in the brackets. We don't need to use an equals operator here, as if there is one it will return *true* and run the line in the brackets, otherwise it'll just carry on with the code.

Line 116: If it finds a sheet called "new", it will delete it using **deleteSheet()**.

```
119.    const newSheet = ss.insertSheet("new");
120.    const newSheetRange = newSheet.getRange(1, 1, 13, 3);
121.    range.copyTo(newSheetRange);
```

Line 119: Now, we're sure we haven't got a sheet called "new", so we can go ahead and insert a sheet called "new".

Line 120: We then get the range on the new sheet. Note, the dimensions of this range need to be the same as the data we're copying, but it could be in different cell locations.

Line 121: We copy the original range to the new range, using **copyTo()**.

```
123.    newSheet.autoResizeColumn(1);
124.    newSheet.setColumnWidth(3, 400);
125.    newSheet.getRange(1, 3, 100).setWrap(true);
126. }
```

Finally, let's format the newly added data a little.

Line 123: First, let's adjust the width of column 1 automatically. Note, this doesn't always adjust the column width snugly to the data, as we'll see, but it's good if you don't know what width your data will need.

Line 124: I'm going to set a specific width of 400 to column 3, using **setColumnWidth()**.

Line 125: As some cells in column C contain a lot of text, I also want to wrap the text in the cells. Here, I've got column 3 and have selected, rather arbitrarily, rows 1 to 100. Then I use **setWrap()** and state *true* to set the text wrap on.

Running the code, we'll see the new sheet has been made, called "new", and we have the first 13 rows added to it, with some basic formatting. Notice, the **copyTo()** method also copied the cell background colours and bolding.

eg7 ▼   new ▼

METHOD	RETURN TYPE	DETAILS
activate()	Range	Make this range the active range.
breakApart()	Range	Break any multi-column cells in the range into individual cells again.
canEdit()	Boolean	Determines whether the user has permission to edit every cell in the range.
clear()	Range	Clears the range of contents, formats, and data-validation rules.
clear(options)	Range	Clears the range of contents, format, data-validation rules, and/or comments, as specified with the given advanced options.
clearContent()	Range	Clears the content of the range, leaving the formatting intact.
clearDataValidations()	Range	Clears the data-validation rules for the range.
clearFormat()	Range	Clears formatting for this range.
clearNote()	Range	Clears the note in the given cell or cells.
copyFormatToRange(gridId, column, columnEnd, row, rowEnd)	void	Copy the formatting of the range to the given location.
copyFormatToRange(sheet, column, columnEnd, row, rowEnd)	void	Copy the formatting of the range to the given location.
copyTo(destination)	void	Copies the data from a range of cells to another range of cells.

There are many methods available in the Range class, allowing you to do most things you want to do. Note, even though there are nearly 200 methods, some are in pairs, get & set, for example, **getBackground()** and **setBackground()**, and some have multiple versions, for example, **clear()** has 6 variants. Enjoy playing around with them!

Find more information on the **Range** class here:

https://developers.google.com/apps-script/reference/spreadsheet/range

Also, you can find information on the **ScriptApp** class and triggers here:

https://developers.google.com/apps-script/reference/script/script-app#newTrigger(String)

Here you can find more information on the **setBorders()** method:

https://developers.google.com/apps-script/reference/spreadsheet/range#setbordertop-left-bottom-right-vertical-horizontal

Plus, there is more information on the **sort()** method in the Google documentation and it has some good, clear examples of how this can be used:

https://developers.google.com/apps-script/reference/spreadsheet/range#sortsortspecobj

You can find the full piece of code for this chapter in Appendix 1.

GOOGLE FORMS

Apps Script with Google Forms

It's common to use Apps Script with both Google Sheets and Forms, as we often get data from a from a form connected to a sheet, or create a form from data in a sheet. If you're starting out I recommend starting in the Sheets part of this before diving into Forms.

What's covered in this part of the book?

Chapter	Apps Script classes and methods	JavaScript concepts
1	FormApp getActiveForm() setTitle()	functions
2	create() addMultipleChoiceItem() setChoiceValues() getItems() asMultipleChoiceItem()	---
3	---	for loop push
4	addTextItem() addDateItem() addDurationItem() addListItem() addScaleItem() setBounds() setLabels() addCheckboxItem() addGridItem() setRows() setColumns() addParagraphItem()	Global variables forEach() Calling functions return if trim data (regular expression) slice() filter() indexOf()

5	MailApp sendEmail() getResponses() getItemResponses() getResponse() getItems() getChoices()	HTML: \<br\> \
6	createTextValidation() setHelpText() requireNumberEqualTo() build() setValidation() setRequired()	---
7	addPageBreakItem() setGoToPage() PageNavigationType.SUBMIT setChoices() createChoice()	---
8	setIsQuiz() setPoints() createFeedback() setText() setFeedbackForCorrect() addLink() setFeedbackForIncorrect()	---

This may not make any sense to you yet, but by the end of the book it will!

Example files and full pieces of code

Links to all the files and full pieces of code used in this part of the book can be found in Appendix 2. The best way to learn is to start using it, so let's jump right in.

CHAPTER 10: First Forms script

In the following chapters, we're going to look at using Apps Script with Google Forms and also, how both Forms and Sheets can work together.

First Google Forms script

Let's look at how we can edit text in a Google Form. Here, we're going to change the title of the form.

Create a new form. At the moment, as it's a new one, the title will just say "Untitled form".

To open the Script editor in Forms, click on the 3 dots menu and then "Script editor".

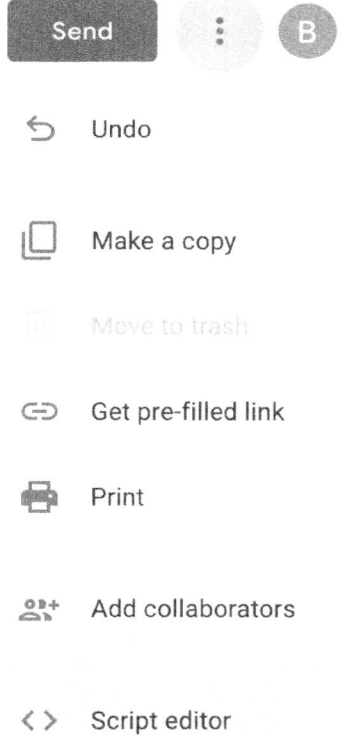

Here we want to edit a form, so we use the **FormApp** class. Type that in and add a dot to bring up the menu.

```
1  function myFunction() {
2      FormApp.
3  }
4
```
- Alignment   interface FormApp.Ali...
- DestinationType
- FeedbackType
- ItemType
- PageNavigationType
- create
- createCheckboxGridValidation
- createCheckboxValidation
- createFeedback
- createGridValidation
- createParagraphTextValidation
- createTextValidation

Now, we want to get this active form, so we scroll down and click on the **getActiveForm()** method.

- getActiveForm

Add a dot and you've guessed it, another menu will appear.

FormApp.getActiveForm().

- setDescription
- setDestination
- setIsQuiz
- setLimitOneResponsePerUser
- setProgressBar
- setPublishingSummary
- setRequireLogin
- setShowLinkToRespondAgain
- setShuffleQuestions
- setTitle
- shortenFormUrl

```
1. function myFunction() {
2.     FormApp.getActiveForm().setTitle("Questionnaire");
3. }
```

Line 2: OK, let's finish off this line. We want to change the title of the form, so we use the **setTitle()** method. Here, I've added "Questionnaire". Then, I end the line with a semi-colon.

Press the Run button on the toolbar to run the program.

▷ Run

The first time you run a script, you will need to authorize it. Click "Review permissions".

Authorization required

This project requires your permission to access your data.

Cancel   Review permissions

Click on the account you're using.

Choose an account

to continue to 1-First Form Script

B **Barrie Roberts**
   bazrobertsbooks@gmail.com

⊙ Use another account

Click "Allow".

1-First Form Script wants to access your Google Account

B bazrobertsbooks@gmail.com

This will allow 1-First Form Script **to:**

● View and manage your forms in Google Drive ⓘ

Make sure you trust 1-First Form Script

You may be sharing sensitive info with this site or app. Learn about how 1-First Form Script will handle your data by reviewing its terms of service and privacy policies. You can always see or remove access in your Google Account.

Learn about the risks

Cancel   **Allow**

You will see the Execution log appear and confirm that it is completed.

Execution log

```
10:59:56 AM    Notice      Execution started
10:59:57 AM    Notice      Execution completed
```

Back on the form, you can see this changed the title from "Untitled form" to "Questionnaire".

Questionnaire

Form description

You can find the full piece of code for this chapter in Appendix 2.

CHAPTER 11: Creating & updating a Google Form

In this chapter, we're going to look at how to create a Google Form with a multiple-choice question. We'll look how you can create the form from data in the script, then look how it can be done taking data from a Google Sheet. In the final example, we'll look at how we can update the question with data from a Sheet.

Example 1 - Creating a Form with a multiple-choice question

Here we're going to create a new form called "New form" and adc the question "Where do you want to go on holiday?" and add two options "Seville" and "London".

```
1. function createForm() {
2.   const form = FormApp.create("New form");
3.   const formQ1 = form.addMultipleChoiceItem();
4.   formQ1.setTitle('Where do you want to go on holiday?');
5.   formQ1.setChoiceValues(['Seville', 'London']);
6. }
```

Let's look at the code line by line:

Line 1: Set up a function called createForm.

Line 2: Use **FormApp** class then the method **create()** with the title of the form in the brackets to create a new form. To then work with it, we store it in the variable *form*.

Line 3: Now, let's add the multiple-choice question. We get the form and then use the **addMultipleChoiceItem()** method. We then store this in the variable *formQ1*, to then add the question and possible options.

Line 4: To add a question, we get the 'multiple-choice item' and use **setTitle()** to set the question.

Lines 5-6: Finally, we need to set the choices that will appear for the question. Use **setChoiceValues()** and in the brackets list the options as an array with a comma between each option. Close the function in line 6.

Run the *createForm* function and the first time authorize the program.

createForm ▼

Authorize the script. In the last chapter, we were able to authorize the script in only 3 steps, but usually if you're using a Gmail account and not an Google Workspace for education or Business account, you need to go through two more steps. Click on Review permissions as before and click on your account.

A scary looking message may appear, which asks you to accept the risks for continuing on or to go back to safety. Don't worry, there's no risk at all as this is your script you're authorizing. Click on "Advanced".

Google hasn't verified this app

The app is requesting access to sensitive info in your Google Account. Until the developer (bazrobertsbooks@gmail.com) verifies this app with Google, you shouldn't use it.

Advanced   BACK TO SAFETY

Then at the bottom, click on the "Go to…" and the name of the script project + (unsafe). It's safe to do so!!

Continue only if you understand the risks and trust the developer (bazrobertsbooks@gmail.com).

Go to 2-FormApp (unsafe)

Then click "Allow".

Your newly-created form will appear in you're my Drive.

 New form

Opening the form, we can see it's given the form a title, added a multiple-choice question and added 2 options.

New form

Form description

Where do you want to go on holiday? — Multiple choice

○ Seville ✕
○ London ✕
○ Add option or add "Other"

Opening the form view we can see the question we've set up.

New form

Where do you want to go on holiday?

○ Seville

○ London

Submit

Example 2 - Creating a Form with data from a Google Sheet

Often you don't want to have to 'hard-wire' the form questions and options, i.e. adding all that information within the script. A more flexible way, is to use a Goog e Sheet and write the question and options there and then get the script to read that information and add it to your form.

Here, we have a page called "newQ".

On the page in column A, we have a question and two options.

	A
1	**Question**
2	Where do you want to go on holiday?
3	**Options**
4	Seville
5	London

The script below is going to get the spreadsheet, get the question and options, then create a form, with a multiple-choice question, using the question and options info from the sheet.

```
8.  function createFormFromData() {
9.    const ss = SpreadsheetApp.getActiveSpreadsheet().getSheetByName("newQ"),
10.         question = ss.getRange(2, 1, 1, 1).getValue(),
11.         options = ss.getRange(4, 1, 2).getValues();
12.
13.    const form = FormApp.create("New form"),
14.         formQ1 = form.addMultipleChoiceItem();
15.    formQ1.setTitle(question);
16.    formQ1.setChoiceValues(options);
17.  }
```

Let's look at it line by line:

Line 8: Create a function called "createFormFromData".

Line 9: Get the active spreadsheet and get the sheet called "newQ". See earlier posts on working with spreadsheets.

Line 10: Get the question from cell A2 (i.e. row 2, column 1) and store it in the variable *question*. Note, here you could actually shorten the getRange part to ss.getRange(**2,1**).getValue() as we are only getting 1 row and 1 column.

Line 11: Get the options from cells A4 and A5 (i.e. rows 4 to 5, column 1) and store it in the array *options*.

Line 13: As we saw before, we use **FormApp** to create the new form.

Line 14: Again as before, we need to add a multiple-choice question.

Line 15: We set the title of the question using the variable *question*.

Lines 16-17: Set the choices using the array *options*, then close the function.

Run the function "createFormFromData".

createFormFromData ▼

The same as before, we get a new form with the question added.

▤ New form

New form

Where do you want to go on holiday?

○ Seville

○ London

Submit

Example 3 - Updating a question in a Form from data in a Google Sheet

We can use similar code to update an already existing Form and change the question and options within that form.

This time our question and options are on a page called "updateQ".

updateQ ▼

Here, we have a different question and 2 different options.

	A
1	**Question**
2	Where did you go on holiday last year?
3	**Options**
4	Málaga
5	Paris

The script is going to get the question and option info as we did before, then it's going to open an existing form, then change the first question to the information we collected from the Sheet.

```
19.    function updateFormFromData() {
20.        const ss =
        SpreadsheetApp.getActiveSpreadsheet().getSheetByName("updateQ"),
21.        question = ss.getRange(2, 1, 1, 1).getValue(),
22.        options = ss.getRange(4, 1, 2).getValues();
23.
24.        const form =
        FormApp.openById('1ANwqzhIGiYQf3a4VBa_Ul2Et16NHwROupCoxURrKPxo'),
25.        allItems = form.getItems(),
26.        formQ1 = allItems[0].asMultipleChoiceItem();
27.        formQ1.setTitle(question);
28.        formQ1.setChoiceValues(options);
29.    }
```

Let's look at it line by line:

Line 19: Set up the function.

Line 20: Get the sheet called "updateQ".

Line 21: Get the question. You could shorten this to ss.getRange(2,1).getValue().

Line 22: Get the options. You could shorten this to ss.getRange(4,1,2).getValues();

Line 24: Get the existing form by opening it by its ID and store it in the *form* variable. You could do the same by getting the form's URL with **openByUrl()**. Obviously, use your own form ID here.

Line 25: This time, we can't just add a multiple-choice item, as we would just create a second question. Instead, we first need to get the number of items in our form. To do so, we use **getItems()**. It gets the items as an array. Here, I've stored it in *allItems*.

Line 26: Now, we need to get our question. It's the first question, so this will be position 0 in our *allItems* array. We need to state what type of question we want. So, here we get it as a multiple-choice item. Note, the difference from the previous example, where we used **add**MultipleChoiceItem().

Line 27: Then, we set the question title as before using **setTitle()** and the *question* variable.

Lines 28-29: Then, we set the options as before using **setChoiceValues()** and the *options* variable. Close the function.

updateFormFromData ▼

Run the function "updateFormFromData".

> **Where did you go on holiday last year?**
> _____
>
> ○ Málaga
>
> ○ Paris
>
> ○ Add option or add "Other"

As we can see, it's changed the question and options in our previous form.

So, as you can see, it's very easy to create questions in a form and to update them from data stored in a Google Sheet.

You can find more information about **item** and its methods here:

https://developers.google.com/apps-script/reference/forms/item

You can find the full pieces of code for this chapter in Appendix 2.

CHAPTER 12: Creating & updating a multiple question Form

Following on from the previous chapter on creating and updating Google Forms, here we'll look at adding and updating **multiple questions** to a form.

Example 1 - Creating multiple questions in a Google Form

Here in a Google Sheet, I have a set of reading comprehension questions, which I want to add to a Google Form. There are 5 questions and each question has 4 multiple-choice options. For simplicity, I've just put options a to d, but you could add different possible answers here, including full sentences. I've also included a row for the answers but in this example we're just setting up the form and won't be using that row.

	A	B	C	D	E	F
1	READING MULTIPLE-CHOICE	Q1	Q2	Q3	Q4	Q5
2	Questions	What is the article about?	What is one of the advantages of going to the UK to learn English?	What is one of the advantages of staying in your country to learn English?	People who don't have a lot of time and money should...	What activity needs a teacher?
3	Possibilities	a	a	a	a	a
4		b	b	b	b	b
5		c	c	c	c	c
6		d	d	d	d	d
7	Answers	d	a	c	b	a

From the Sheet, open the Script Editor.

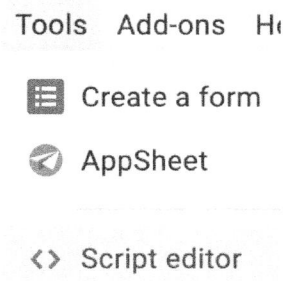

The code we're going to write is going to get the data from Sheet1, then store the questions and options in variables. Then it's going to create a new form and add those questions and options to it.

Let's look at it line by line.

150

```
1.  function createFormFromData() {
2.    const sh = SpreadsheetApp.getActiveSpreadsheet().getSheetByName("Sheet1");
3.  //Get data, number of questions and options info
4.    const data = sh.getDataRange().getValues(),
5.    numOfOptions = data.length-3,
6.    numOfQs = data[0].length;
```

Line 1: Set up a function called "createFormFromData()".

Line 2: Get the sheet called "Sheet1" and store it in the variable *sh*.

Line 5: Get all the data on the sheet using the **getDataRange()** method and store it in *data*.

Here's what the contents of *data* looks like.

[[READING MULTIPLE-CHOICE, Q1, Q2, Q3, Q4, Q5], [Questions, What is the article about?, What is one of the advantages of going to the UK to learn English?, What is one of the advantages of staying in your country to learn English?, People who don't have a lot of time and money should..., What activity needs a teacher?], [Possibilities, a, a, a, a], [, b, b, b, b, b], [, c, c, c, c, c], [, d, d, c, d, d], [Answers, d, a, c, b, a]]

Line 6: We need to know how many options there are. Getting the **length** of the array data, we will see there are 7 rows but we are only interested in the options, so we subtract 3 as there are 3 rows that are not needed (header, questions, and answer rows), leaving us with the number of options.

Line 7: Now, we need the number of questions. We can use the **length** method again, but this time we're not interested in the rows, but the columns. So, we look at the first row of data in our array by stating 'row 0' and then get the length of it.

Then, store it in the *numOfQs* variable. This will find 6 columns, which is 1 more than the number of questions we have but we'll deal with that later.

```
9.   //Get questions
10.    const questions = sh.getRange(2, 2, 1, numOfQs).getValues();
```

Line 10: Now, let's get the questions and add all of them in one go to an array called *questions*. We do this by getting the range of cells from row 2, column 2, up until the last column, which is the number we just worked out in *numOfQs*. Remember to get the values in those cells.

[[What is the article about?, What is one of the advantages of going to the UK to learn English?, What is one of the advantages of staying in your country to learn English?, People who don't have a lot of time and money should..., What activity needs a teacher?,]]

Here, we can see the 5 questions stored in the *questions* array.

```
12.     //Get options and store in an array
13.     var allOptions = [];
14.     for (q=2;q<=numOfQs;q++){
15.       let options = sh.getRange(3, q, numOfOptions).getValues();
16.       allOptions.push(options);
17.     }
```

Now, we need to get the options for each question, and store them in an array, so that question 1's options are stored together, then question 2's, and so on.

Line 13: First, let's create an empty array, where we're going to store the options and call it *allOptions*.

Line 14: We're going to need to loop through the options, so set up a **for loop** and start at column 2 and end at the final column (*numOfQs*). So, basically, it will get the data from the 5 question columns.

Line 15: Each time around the loop, it will get the list of options, starting from row 3, column q, and the number of rows is dictated by the number of options we found out earlier, in *numOfOptions* variable. And finally, we're only getting 1 column each time we go around.

Line 16: We then need to push that set of data into our empty array. To do so, we use the **push** method and pass the data stored in *options* into it.

[[[a], [b], [c], [d]], [[a], [b], [c], [d]], [[a], [b], [c], [d]], [[a], [b], [c], [d]], [[a], [b], [c], [d]]]

This is what the data in *allOptions* looks like. We can see it's got all 5 sets of options and grouped them by question (notice the double squared brackets).

```
19.     //Create the form
20.     const form = FormApp.create("New form");
```

Line 20: Then, we create a new form.

Finally, we need to add the questions and the options to our newly-created form.

```
22.     //Add questions and options to form
23.     for (qq=0;qq<numOfQs-1;qq++){
```

```
24.        let formQ = form.addMultipleChoiceItem();
25.        formQ.setTitle(questions[0][qq]);
26.        formQ.setChoiceValues(allOptions[qq]);
27.    }
28. }
```

Line 23: We're going to loop through the questions and *allOptions* arrays. We set up a for loop and as we're looping through arrays, our starting point is 0 (i.e. the first position) and we want to loop through the number of questions there are, which is *numOfQs*-1 as originally, we included the first column in our sheet, which we need to ignore.

Line 24: During each loop, we first need to add a multiple-choice question, using the **addMultipleChoiceItem()** method to our form.

Line 25: Then, we need to set the question using the **setTitle()** method. We get the question from the *questions* array and as we only have 1 'row' in the array, we use [0] first and then use the counter *qq* to move long the array each time.

Line 26: Finally, we need to add the options by using the **setChoiceValues()** method. We get the options from the *allOptions* array using the counter *qq* to get the appropriate set of options.

Run the script.

 New form

In your My Drive you'll find the new form.

New form

Form description

What is the article about?

○ a

○ b

○ c

○ d

What is one of the advantages of going to the UK to learn English?

○ a

○ b

○ c

○ d

...

Opening it, we can see it's been populated with our questions and options.

Example 2 - Updating multiple questions in a Google Form

This time let's update an existing form. Note, this script is to update a form with the same number of questions and options. I use this type of code for exams that are in a set format so, the number of questions is the same but of course, the content is different, but the number of options is also the same.

Here on Sheet2 we have a similar set of data, but this time I've decided I want to rearrange the questions and I want to change the options from letters to numbers. You of course, could use this to use different questions and possible answers.

	A	B	C	D	E	F
1	READING MULTIPLE-CHOICE	Q1	Q2	Q3	Q4	Q5
2	Questions	What activity needs a teacher?	What is one of the advantages of staying in your country to learn English?	What is the article about?	What is one of the advantages of going to the UK to learn English?	People who don't have a lot of time and money should...
3	Possibilities	1	1	1	1	1
4		2	2	2	2	2
5		3	3	3	3	3
6		4	4	4	4	4
7	Answers	4	1	3	2	1

The first part of this code is similar to above but from line 49, we're getting an existing form and updating it with the questions and options from the table above.

Let's look at it line by line, although as the top part is basically the same as above, I will briefly go through those parts.

```
30.   function updateFormFromData() {
31.     const sh =
      SpreadsheetApp.getActiveSpreadsheet().getSheetByName("Sheet2");
```

Lines 30-31: Set up the new function and get "Sheet2".

```
33.   //Get data, number of questions and options info
34.   const data = sh.getDataRange().getValues(),
35.       numOfOptions = data.length-3,
36.       numOfQs = data[0].length;
```

Lines 33-36: Get the data on Sheet2, the number of questions and options that we're going to work with.

```
38.   //Get questions
39.   const questions = sh.getRange(2, 2, 1, numOfQs).getValues();
```

Line 39: Get the questions and store them in the *questions* array.

```
41.   //Get options and store in an array
42.   var allOptions = [];
43.     for (q=2;q<=numOfQs;q++){
44.       let options = sh.getRange(3, q, numOfOptions).getValues();
45.       allOptions.push(options);
46.     }
```

Lines 42-46: Get the options for each question and store them in blocks in the *allOptions* variable.

```
48.    //Get existing form
49.    const form = FormApp.openById('FORM ID'),
50.      allItems = form.getItems();
```

Line 49: This time, let's get a form I've already created by its ID. (Insert your own form ID here).

Line 50: Then, get the number of items (in this case just questions) already in the form, using **getItems()**.

```
52.    //Add questions and options to form
53.    for (qq=0;qq<numOfQs-1;qq++){
54.      let formQ = allItems[qq].asMultipleChoiceItem();
55.      formQ.setTitle(questions[0][qq]);
56.      formQ.setChoiceValues(allOptions[qq]);
57.    }
58.  }
```

Line 53: We're going to loop through the data five times (i.e. the number of questions: *numOfQs*-1).

Line 54: We then need to set the existing questions as multiple-choice questions using this time **asMultipleChoiceItem()**.

Line 55: Then, we set the questions, using **setTitle()** as before, looping through the *questions* array.

Line 56: Finally, set the choices using **setChoiceValues()** and looping through the *allOptions* array.

Run the script.

New form

Form description

What activity needs a teacher?

○ 1

○ 2

○ 3

○ 4

What is one of the advantages of staying in your country to learn English?

○ 1

○ 2

○ 3

○ 4

...

As you can see it's updated the form with the new questions and numbered answers.

It's very easy to make and update forms using data from Google Sheets and usually quicker and easier to do than manually making the questions directly on the forms.

You can find the full pieces of code for this chapter in Appendix 2.

CHAPTER 13: Adding different types of questions to a form

In this chapter, we're going to look at how we can add different types of questions to a Google Form from a Google Sheet. As an example, we're going to create a questionnaire with 9 different question types.

Questionnaire	Question type	Questions
Q1	text	Name
Q2	date	Course start
Q3	duration	Course length
Q4	multiplec	Level
Q5	list	Teacher
Q6	scale	Did you enjoy the classes?
Q7	checkbox	Services used
Q8	grid	Please give feedback on the following areas
Q9	paragraph	Comments

In our sheet we have the questions and various options we're going to use. Column B has the question types, which will tell our script which type of question to set up. Column C has the questions.

D	E	F	G	H	I	J	K
Options							
A1	A2	B1					
Fred	Wilma	Barney	Betty				
1	5	Not at all	Absolutely				
Language exchange	Book shop	Multimedia room					
Signing up process	Classes	Services provided	Cultural activities	**Columns:**	Poor	Average	Excellent

Columns D to K, contain the various options for each question.

Overview of script

Our script will:

1. Create a form

2. Get the data from the sheet
3. Loop down each row checking the type of question
4. Run the appropriate function to make the corresponding question and options

Here, we're also going to learn how we can use the **forEach()**, **slice()**, **indexOf()**, and **filter()** methods.

Creating a new Google Form

```
1. //Create new form - Global variable so it can be seen by all functions
2. const FORM = FormApp.create("Questionnaire");
```

Line 2: Create a new form using **FormApp**. I've put it outside the main function to create a **global variable** so that the form is visible throughout the script and in the different functions. Here, it's stored in the constant *FORM*.

Getting the data from the sheet

```
4. function makeQuestionnaire() {
5. //Get data and last row from spreadsheet
6. const sh = SpreadsheetApp.getActiveSpreadsheet().getSheetByName("Sheet1"),
7.     data = sh.getDataRange().getValues();
```

Line 4: Set up the main function, *makeQuestionnaire*.

Line 6: Get the sheet called "Sheet1", where the questions are stored.

Line 7: Get all the data on the sheet, using **getDataRange()** and **getValues()**, then store it in the variable, *data*.

Note, with this we're only making one call to the Sheet as we'll then be working with the *data* array, so, this will make the code run much faster than getting the data bit by bit from the sheet.

Looping down the rows of questions

```
10.    //Loop through each question and check what question type it is
11.      data.forEach(checkQuestionType)
12.    }
```

Line 11: Now, we need to loop through the questions. To do this, we can use the **forEach()** method, which loops through all the items in an array and runs the function named in the brackets. So, here it will get the items in the *data* array (i.e. the rows on the sheet), then run the function called *checkQuestionType*, which will do just that, check the question type and set up the appropriate question.

Checking the question type

Above we referred to a function to check the question type, so let's set that up now.

```
14.    //function to check question type
15.    function checkQuestionType(data){
16.      if(data[1] === "text"){
17.      makeTextQ(data);
18.    }
```

Line 15: Set up the function and pass the data from the variable *data* into it.

Line 16: Now, we check the type of question. The question will be in position 1 of the array data (i.e. column B). So, we check if data[1] equals "text". Note, as we are using the **forEach()** method, we don't need to state the row, as this is already known as it loops down the rows.

Line 17: If the question type is text, we run the function called *makeTextQ()* and pass the *data* variable to it.

Line 18: Close the function.

```
19.      else if(data[1] === "date"){
20.        makeDateQ(data);
21.      }
22.      else if(data[1] === "duration"){
23.        makeDurationQ(data);
24.      }
25.      else if(data[1] === "multiplec"){
```

```
26.        makeMultipleCQ(data);
27.     }
28.     else if(data[1] === "list"){
29.        makeListQ(data);
30.     }
31.     else if(data[1] === "scale"){
32.        makeScaleQ(data);
33.     }
34.     else if(data[1] === "checkbox"){
35.        makeCheckboxQ(data);
36.     }
37.     else if(data[1] === "grid"){
38.        makeGridQ(data);
39.     }
40.     else if(data[1] === "paragraph"){
41.        makeParagraphQ(data);
42.     }
43. }
```

Lines 19 to 43: We do the same for each of the question types. We check the question type then if it matches, we run the function associated with that question type.

Functions to make the questions

In the final part, we set up the functions for each of the question types. The basic format for most question types, is to **add** the question **item**, then **set** its **title**.

Making a text question

The only information we need for a text question is the question title, which is in the third column.

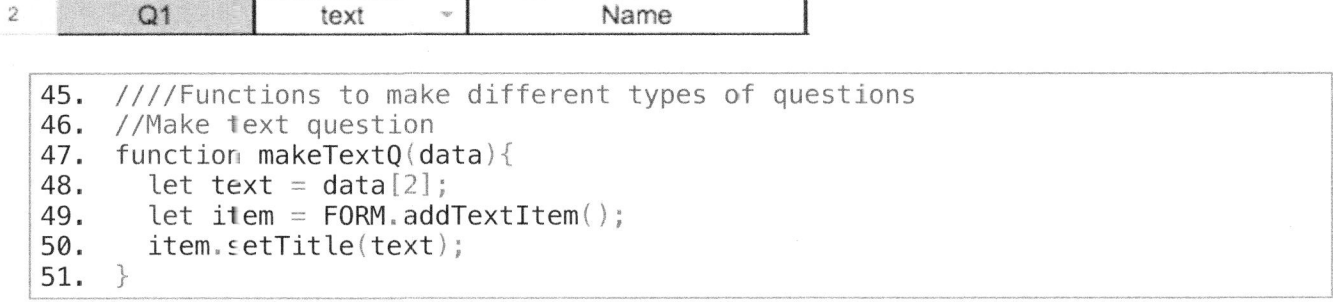

```
45. ////Functions to make different types of questions
46. //Make text question
47. function makeTextQ(data){
48.    let text = data[2];
49.    let item = FORM.addTextItem();
50.    item.setTitle(text);
51. }
```

Line 47: Set up a function called *makeTextQ()* and pass the *data* variable to it.

Line 48: Get the question title, which is in position 2 of the *data* array (i.e. the third column).

Line 49: Get the form and add the text item to it. Store this in the *item* variable.

Line 50: Set the question title, using the information in the *text* variable.

Line 51: Close the function.

Making a date question

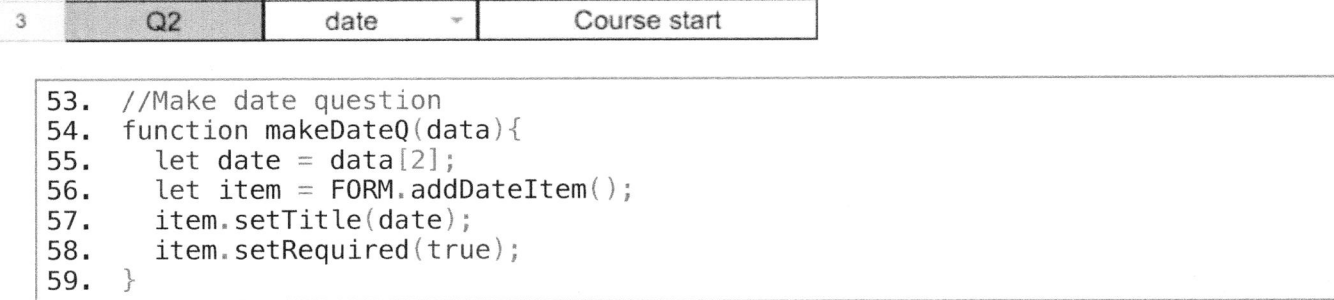

```
53.    //Make date question
54.    function makeDateQ(data){
55.       let date = data[2];
56.       let item = FORM.addDateItem();
57.       item.setTitle(date);
58.       item.setRequired(true);
59.    }
```

Lines 54-57: This is exactly the same as the function above to make a text question, except that we need to add a date item, so we use **addDateItem()** in line 56.

Line 58: I've added an extra line, showing how we can also set questions to be required to be filled out. This is simply done with the **setRequired()** method on the item and stating *true* in the brackets. This of course is optional.

Making a duration question

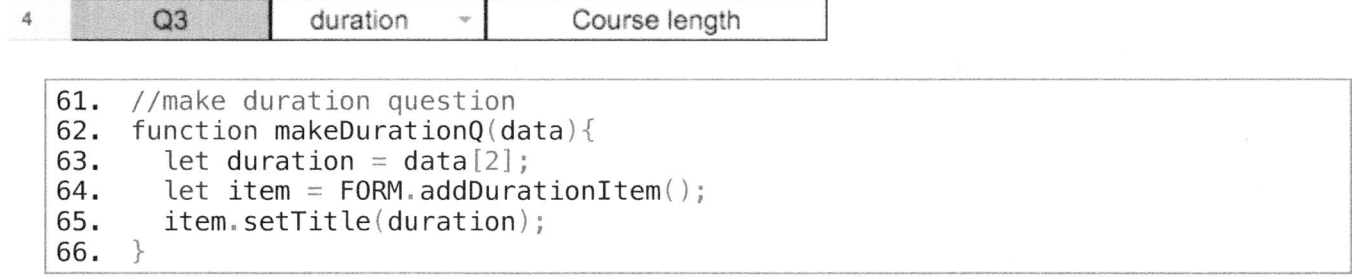

```
61.    //make duration question
62.    function makeDurationQ(data){
63.       let duration = data[2];
64.       let item = FORM.addDurationItem();
65.       item.setTitle(duration);
66.    }
```

Lines 62-66: Again, adding a duration question is similar to adding a text question, you just need to use the **addDurationItem()** method.

Making a multiple-choice question

Adding a multiple-choice question is a bit more complex than adding just a text question, as we also have to add the possible options. As I've set up the sheet to allow the user to add however many options they want, we need to also to know how many options there are and to ignore any blank cells.

In this example, we have a question asking for the student's "Level" and then 3 options, A1, A2, and B1. After the options there are blank cells, which we'll need to ignore otherwise we'll add blank options to our question on the form.

| Q4 | multiplec ▾ | Level | A1 | A2 | B1 |

The first part of this function is similar to the text one, in that we're going to get the question, add the item to the form and set the question title.

```
68.   //make Multiple-Choice question
69.   function makeMultipleCQ(data){
70.     let mcQuestion = data[2];
71.     let item = FORM.addMultipleChoiceItem();
72.     item.setTitle(mcQuestion);
```

Line 69: Set up the function called *makeMultipleCQ()* and pass the *data* variable into it.

Line 70: Get the question from the *data* variable.

Line 71: Add the multiple-choice item to the form.

Line 72: Set the question title using the *mcQuestion* variable.

At the moment, the *data* variable contains the whole row of data, which may also include some blank cells at the end. In our example, this is the content of data for this particular row:

```
[Q4, multiplec, Level, A1, A2, B1, , , , , ]
```

As we don't want blank options on our form, we're going to need to get rid of them. To do this, we're going to use a combination of an array filter and function to look for spaces and if it finds any it filters them out.

I've taken this piece of code from the **StackOverflow** site (the URL is at the end of this chapter), and it's an example of where you can find useful pieces of code without having to try to invent it yourself. It's also something that even if you don't fully understand the details of it, you can see how it works and so use it as a complete block of code.

```
74.   //Getting options
75.   let trimmedData = data.filter(function(str) {
76.     return /\S/.test(str);
77.   });
```

Line 75: We get the data array and use the filter method. Then we set up a function with the parameter called *str*. We'll store the end result in the variable *trimmedData*.

Line 76: In our function, we're going to test to see if there is a space in the array. We use the **test()** method to do that and we look for a space by using the **regular expression /\S/**. If the returned result is true, i.e. it's found a space, it filters it out of the array.

Line 77: Close the function.

```
[Q4, multiplec, Level, A1, A2, B1]
```

If we ran it and logged it, we can see it's got rid of those spaces at the end. Now, we need to get just the options from our row.

```
78.   //Getting options without spaces
79.   let slicedData = trimmedData.slice(3,trimmedData.length);
```

Line 79: Using the variable *trimmedData*, use the **slice** method to get certain values in our array. We need the values from position 3 until the end of the array. So, in the brackets we state 3 (starting position), and use the **length** method to find the end of our array.

```
[A1, A2, B1]
```

As you can see above it's just left with the options.

```
81.   //Adding option to Form
82.     item.setChoiceValues(slicedData);
83.   }
```

Line 82: Finally, we add this sliced data into the options for our multiple-choice question, by using **setChoiceValues()**.

Making a list question

This is almost exactly the same as creating a multiple-choice question, except that in line 88 we use the **addListItem()** method.

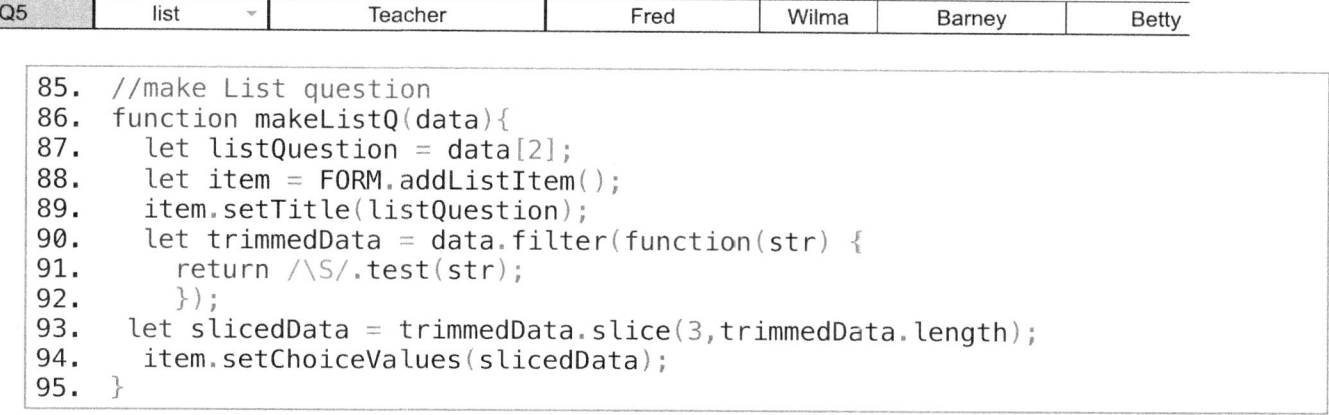

```
85.    //make List question
86.    function makeListQ(data){
87.       let listQuestion = data[2];
88.       let item = FORM.addListItem();
89.       item.setTitle(listQuestion);
90.       let trimmedData = data.filter(function(str) {
91.          return /\S/.test(str);
92.       });
93.       let slicedData = trimmedData.slice(3,trimmedData.length);
94.       item.setChoiceValues(slicedData);
95.    }
```

Making a scale question

A scale question is where you have a scale, for example 1 to 5, and the user clicks on a number. So, we need to set the bottom end and the top end of the scale. Plus, we have the option of adding labels to that scale, indicating what the numbers mean, for example, "bad" to "excellent".

In our example, we have a question "Did you enjoy the classes?", then have a scale 1 to 5, and we're going to label the scale, so that 1 is "Not at all" and 5 is "Absolutely". The layout on the sheet is as follows:

| Q6 | scale | Did you enjoy the classes? | 1 | 5 | Not at all | Absolutely |

The first part where we set the question title is the same as we've seen before, except that we're going to use the **addScaleItem()** method in line 101.

165

```
98.   //make Scale question
99.   function makeScaleQ(data){
100.    let scaleQ = data[2];
101.    let item = FORM.addScaleItem();
102.    item.setTitle(scaleQ);
```

I've included the trimming of the blank cells here, but in reality, it's not required as we're going to use specific cells to get our scale and labels, but I've left it in anyway, and as you can see it's identical to the code we saw in the multiple-choice question.

```
104.  let trimmedData = data.filter(function(str) {
105.    return /\S/.test(str);
106.  });
```

The final part is different as this is where we will get the scale and the labels.

```
108.    //Get and set lower and upper bounds of scale
109.    let lower = trimmedData.slice(3, 4);
110.    let upper = trimmedData.slice(4, 5);
111.    item.setBounds(lower, upper);
112.    //Set labels to lower and upper bounds
113.    item.setLabels(trimmedData.slice(5, 6), trimmedData.slice(6, 7));
114.  }
```

Line 109: Get the lower end of the scale, which in our example is the "1". We do this by getting position 3 in our *trimmedData* array using the **slice()** method. This will return the one figure.

Line 110: We do the same for the upper end of the scale, this time getting position 4.

Line 111: Now, we need to set the bounds of our scale, by using **setBounds()** and adding the two figures we just collected.

Line 113: Finally, we set the labels similar to the way we got the scale bounds. We get the lower label from position 5 and the upper label from position 6.

Note, here I've not added them to variables first like the *lower* and *upper* values, I've directly put them in the brackets. You could do the same in line 111 and in the brackets put the trimmedData and slice parts there, to save a couple of lines of code.

Line 114: Close the function.

Making a checkbox question

This is essentially the same as the multiple-choice question, with the only difference being the **addCheckboxItem()** method in line 119.

| Q7 | checkbox | Services used | Language exchange | Book shop | Multimedia room |

```
116. //make Checkbox question
117. function makeCheckboxQ(data){
118.   let checkboxQ = data[2];
119.   let item = FORM.addCheckboxItem();
120.   item.setTitle(checkboxQ);
121.   let trimmedData = data.filter(function(str) {
122.     return /\S/.test(str);
123.   });
124.   let slicedData = trimmedData.slice(3,trimmedData.length);
125.   item.setChoiceValues(slicedData);
126. }
```

Making a grid question

A grid question is where there is a row of options and a column of options and the user selects from several options, for example, giving their opinion on several topics.

Please give feedback on the following areas

	Poor	Average	Excellent
Signing up process	○	○	○
Classes	○	○	○
Services provided	○	○	○
Cultural activities	○	○	○

On our sheet, I've added the question title in column C, as per the other questions. Then, the rows are next, in this case there are 4 options. Then, I've included a cell, "Columns:" telling the user where the column options start, but which I will also use in the code to tell the script, where to get the column options. Then, the column options are to the right of it.

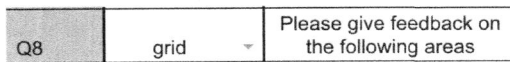

The first part is the same as we've seen before, except we use the **addGridItem()** method in line 131.

```
128.   //make Grid question
129.   function makeGridQ(data){
130.     let gridQ = data[2];
131.     let item = FORM.addGridItem();
132.     item.setTitle(gridQ);
```

As the number of options could vary, we could also have blank cells, which we need to get rid of, so we use the same filter method as we saw earlier.

```
134.   let trimmedData = data.filter(function(str) {
135.     return /\S/.test(str);
136.   });
```

Now, we need to find where the column options start and where the row options finish. We will use the cell called "Columns:" to do this for us.

```
138.   //Find where "Columns:" text is in array
139.   let columnPosition = trimmedData.indexOf("Columns:");
```

Line 139: We can find the position of a specific item by using the **indexOf()** method. This will look for the item stated in the brackets, in this case the text "Columns:" and return the position of it in the array as a number. We'll store that in the variable *columnPosition*, to be used below.

```
141.   //Get row values for grid
142.   let slicedDataRows = trimmedData.slice(3,columnPosition);
143.   //Get column values for grid
144.   let slicedDataColumns =
       trimmedData.slice(columnPosition+1,trimmedData.length);
```

Line 142: We get the row options by slicing the *trimmedData* array. We start at position 3 (column D) and get the values up to but not including the position of the "Columns:" text.

Line 144: Next, we get the column options by slicing the *trimmedData* array. We start at the position after the "Columns:" text, so *columnPosition+1*, and get the values up to the end of the *trimmedData* array, using the **length** method to determine the end of the array.

```
146.    item.setRows(slicedDataRows);
147.    item.setColumns(slicedDataColumns);
148. }
```

Line 146: To add the rows to our grid question, we use the **setRows()** method and pass the *slicedDataRows* variable we just set up.

Line 147: We do the same for the columns, this time using the **setColumns()** method.

Making a paragraph question

This is like the text question we started with, except for the use of the **addParagraphTextItem()** method in line 153.

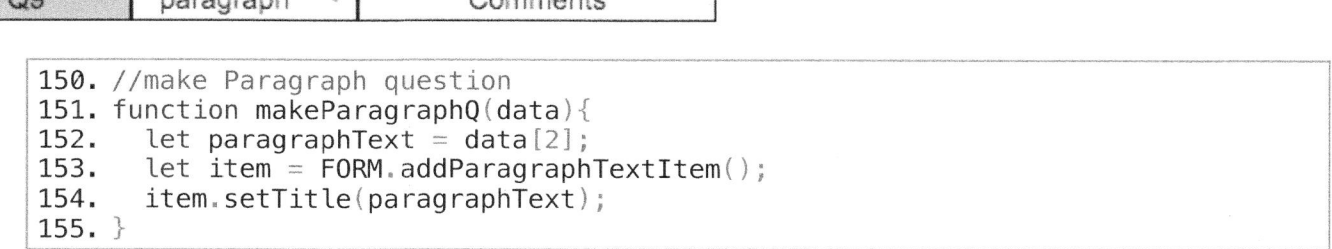

```
150. //make Paragraph question
151. function makeParagraphQ(data){
152.    let paragraphText = data[2];
153.    let item = FORM.addParagraphTextItem();
154.    item.setTitle(paragraphText);
155. }
```

Running the code

Now, we're ready to run our code and set up the questionnaire. Select the "makeQuestionnaire" function and click play. The first time you run it, you'll have to go through the permissions screens.

makeQuestionnaire ▼

As we can see it's created our questionnaire in our My Drive.

☰   Questionnaire

Opening the file up in view mode, we can see the different questions it's set up:

Questionnaire

* Required

Name

Your answer

Course start *

Date

dd/mm/yyyy

Course length

Hrs   Min   Sec

   :   :

Level

○ A1

○ A2

○ B1

Teacher

Choose ▼

Did you enjoy the classes?

	1	2	3	4	5	
Not at all	○	○	○	○	○	Absolutely

Services used

- ☐ Language exchange
- ☐ Book shop
- ☐ Multimedia room

Please give feedback on the following areas

	Poor	Average	Excellent
Signing up process	○	○	○
Classes	○	○	○
Services provided	○	○	○
Cultural activities	○	○	○

Comments

Your answer

Note, this example has a different question type for each question, but you can have multiple questions with the same question type and can leave some of the question types out. I also added some data validation to the question column, so that the question types can be selected from a drop-down menu, allowing it to be entered quicker and ensuring the types were correctly entered.

The good thing about this piece of code is that you can easily create different types of forms with the same piece of code, and all you need to do is set up the Google Sheet with the question types, questions and options and the code will do the rest.

Further information

For further information on some of the methods we used in this code, check out the W3Schools site:

forEach()

https://www.w3schools.com/JSREF/jsref_forEach.asp

slice()

https://www.w3schools.com/jsref/jsref_slice_array.asp

indexOf()

https://www.w3schools.com/jsref/jsref_indexof_array.asp

filter()

https://www.w3schools.com/jsref/jsref_filter.asp

Regular Expressions

https://www.w3schools.com/jsref/jsref_obj_regexp.asp

You can find the full pieces of code for this chapter in Appendix 1.

Stackoverflow – Removing whitespaces in arrays

https://stackoverflow.com/questions/20668872/remove-whitespace-only-array-elements

CHAPTER 14: Using Form responses

In the previous chapters, we looked at how we can create Google Forms from Google Sheets. This time, we're going to look at how we can work with the **responses** a form user submits.

We'll look at two main ways:

1) Getting the form responses from a Google Sheet

2) Getting the form responses directly from a Google Form.

To show some practical uses of this, we'll do the following:

1. Set up a simple **problem-reporting log**, which will email the relevant parties the problem in a classroom. We'll do this via the Sheet and via the Form.
2. Get students' pieces of writing submitted via a Google Form and copy them to their **individual sheets**, ready to have feedback added.
3. Set up a simple **appointment system**, which will update itself as people take the appointments, leaving only the available ones on the Form.

Example 1a - Problem-reporting log & email (Sheet version)

Here, we have a Google Form, which a teacher can fill in if they have a problem in their classroom. They fill in the problem and click on the classroom, then submit the form.

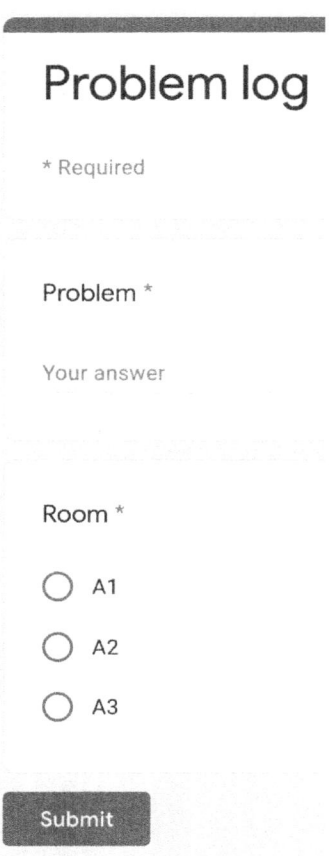

The Form is linked to a Google Sheet and the form response is stored on the sheet called 'Form Responses 1". This is where we'll get the response and then email it to the IT department, so they can come and sort the problem out.

	A	B	C
1	Timestamp	Problem	Room
2	18/03/2021 08:43:03	PC doesn't turn on	A2

The Code

The code will get the form submission from the Sheet, then create an email containing the information from the submission, then email it to the relevant people.

```
1.  function sendProblem() {
2.    const ss = SpreadsheetApp.getActiveSpreadsheet(),
3.      fr = ss.getSheetByName("Form Responses 1"),
4.      lastRowValues = fr.getRange(fr.getLastRow(), 1, 1,
      fr.getLastColumn()).getValues(),
5.      problem = lastRowValues[0][1],
6.      room = lastRowValues[0][2];
```

Line 1: Set up the function.

Line 2: Get the active spreadsheet.

Line 3: Get the sheet where the responses are and store it in the variable *fr*.

Line 4: We're interested in just the final row, which is the latest response. So, we get the range (lastRow, first column, 1 row, to the last column), then get the values on that row.

Line 5: First, we want the problem submitted, which is in column B (array position 1).

Line 6: Secondly, we want the room, which is in column C (array position 2).

Now, let's create the email. It has 3 parts: email subject, who you're sending it to, email body. We'll assign them to 3 variables, *emailSubject*, *emailTo*, and *emailBody*.

```
8.  //Create email
9.  const emailSubject = "Problem",
10.       emailTo = 'brgablog@gmail.com, brgablog2@gmail.com',
11.       emailBody = "Problem: " + problem + "<br /> \
12.    Room: " + room;
```

Line 9: Let's state the subject as "Problem".

Line 10: We're going to send it to two people, so we wrap the email addresses in quotes marks.

Finally, we need to create the body, which will contain the information from our form submission. I want one line with the problem and the other with the room.

Line 11: We add the text "Problem: " then add the variable *problem*, which will add the submitted problem. At the end I've added a HTML line break <br />. Use a backslash to show the next line is connected to this one.

Line 12: Then, we add the text "Room: " and add the variable *room*.

```
14.  //Send email
15.  MailApp.sendEmail(emailTo,emailSubject,'',{
16.    htmlBody: emailBody});
17. }
```

The final part is to send the email. This will use the 3 components above.

Lines 15-16: As this is a basic email, let's use the **MailApp** service and the **sendEmail()** method. In the brackets we need to pass the 3 components we created earlier. The email addresses we're sending to, the email subject, the third parameters, we leave a blank pair of quote marks, as the email body will be set by a little bit of HTML. I've included a bit of HTML, so we'll have to use the **htmlBody** object, which is added between the curly brackets and its value is the *emailBody* variable we set up.

To make this run automatically when a teacher fills in the form, we need to set up a trigger, which will run the code when a form is submitted.

 Triggers

Click on Triggers from the menu on the left-hand side.

To add a new trigger, click on "Add Trigger".

Choose which function to run

sendProblem

Failure notification settings

Notify me immediately

Which runs at deployment

Head

Select event source

From spreadsheet

Select event type

On form submit

Select "sendProblem", "From spreadsheet" and "On form submit" from the drop-down menus and click Save. This will add the trigger.

Authorize the script, then fill in the form and submit it and as you can see, it's emailed the appropriate people with the problem and room.

Problem

bazrobertsbooks@gmail.com
to brgablog, brgablog2

Problem: PC doesn't turn on
Room: A2

Simple, yet so effective and quicker and easier than writing out an email every time.

Example 1b - Problem-reporting log & email (Form version)

Now, let's look at how we can do the same thing but this time get the form response information <u>directly from the form</u> and send the email from within Forms, without the need of a Google Sheet. The form is the same format we used above.

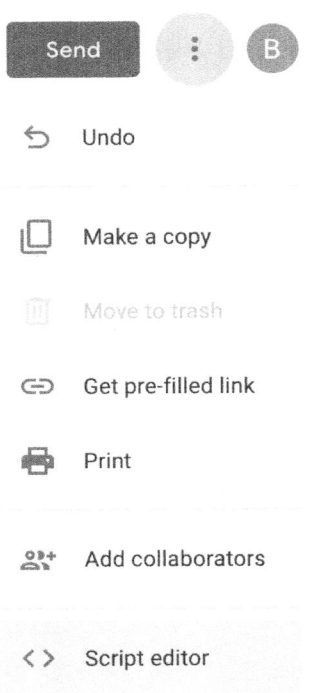

From the form, click on the 3-dots menu and select the Script Editor.

The Code

The first part of the code will be different from that above.

```
1. function sendProblemFromForm() {
2. //Get submitted problem and room from form
3.   const form = FormApp.getActiveForm(),
4.     formResponses = form.getResponses(),
5.     latestFR = formResponses[form.getResponses().length-1];
```

Line 1: Set up the function.

Line 3: Get the active form using **FormApp**.

Line 4: First, we get all the responses form the form, using **getResponses()**. We'll store those in *formResponses*.

Line 5: Now, let's get the latest form response. We just get the last response in the *formResponses* array, using the length of the array to find the last one. We minus one as it's an array.

getResponses() makes an array of all the responses from that form. **getResponses()[n]** gets the responses from the nth submission, for example, the latest submission.

We then need to get the response for each individual question within that submission. We do that by getting the **itemResponses()** for that submission, then getting a response for a particular position within that array.

```
7.    const itemResponses = latestFR.getItemResponses(),
8.        problem = itemResponses[0].getResponse(),
9.        room = itemResponses[1].getResponse();
```

Line 7: First, we get all the responses for the latest form submission and store it in the array, *itemResponses*.

Line 8: Now, we just pick the particular question response we want. The 'problem' is the first question, so will be *itemResponses[0]* and then we get the response.

Line 9: We do the same for the room, except this is the second question, i.e. *itemResponses[1]*.

Lines 11-20 are identical to what we saw in the previous example.

```
11.   //Create email
12.     const emailSubject = "Problem",
13.        emailTo = 'brgablog@gmail.com, brgablog2@gmail.com',
14.        emailBody = "Problem: " + problem + "<br /> \
15.        Room: " + room;
16.
17.   //Send email
18.   MailApp.sendEmail(emailTo,emailSubject,'',{
19.        htmlBody: emailBody});
20.   }
```

We set up a trigger again, with the drop-down menus as in the previous example.

When the form is submitted, it will send an email as we saw in the previous example, except without the need to register the response on the Google Sheet.

Example 2 - Move students' pieces of writing to their individual sheets

Google Forms is great for receiving students' work but if you use the same form for all your students, all that work appears on the same sheet and you may not want to share that with your students. A simple solution is to have a separate sheet for each student, where all their work is in one place, which you could share or send to them.

Here, we're going to set up a simple way for the script to get the latest form submission and to copy it to the student's individual sheet. The main idea of this script is to show how easy this is and I'm sure you could think of other applications for your own situation.

We have a form where the student selects their name from a drop-down list and fills in their piece of writing. I highly recommend using a list instead of the student typing in their name, not just because it's quicker for them but more importantly it makes sure the format of their name is correct, as we're going to use this to move their submission. A simple typo would stop this working.

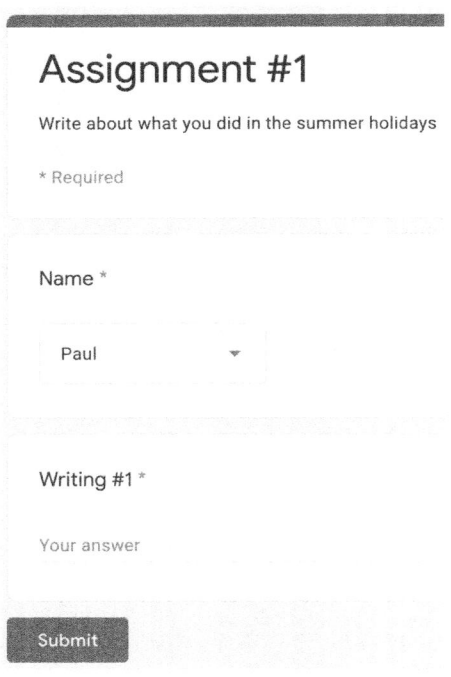

On the Google Sheet we have 5 pages, the form responses sheet called "Assignment1" and the sheets for each of the students.

Their submissions appear on the "Assignment1" sheet.

	A	B	C
1	Timestamp	Name	Writing #1
2	19/03/2021 10:31:40	John	I played my guitar and sang a bit.
3	20/03/2021 10:11:14	Paul	I wrote some songs. One day I want to be a famous pop star.
4			

The script then appends them to their individual sheets:

	A	B	C	D
1	Timestamp	Name	Writing	Feedback
2	20/10/2017 10:11:14	Paul	I wrote some songs. One day I want to be a famous pop star.	
3				

	A	B	C	D
1	Timestamp	Name	Writing	Feedback
2	19/10/2017 10:31:40	John	I played my guitar and sang a bit.	
3				

The Code

```
1. function assignments() {
2.   const ss = SpreadsheetApp.getActiveSpreadsheet();
```

Lines 1-2: Set the function up and get the active spreadsheet.

```
4. //Get assignment
5.   const fr = ss.getSheetByName("Assignment1");
6.   const lastRowValues = fr.getRange(fr.getLastRow(), 1, 1,
   fr.getLastColumn()).getValues();
```

Line 5: Get the form responses sheet.

Line 6: Get the latest form submission, which is on the last row.

```
8. //Get the sheet of the student who's just submitted and append their
   assignment on that sheet
9.   const sheets = ss.getSheets();
10.    for (var sh = 0 ; sh < sheets.length ; sh++) {
11.      let sheetName = sheets[sh].getSheetName();
12.      if(lastRowValues[0][1] === sheetName){
13.   ss.getSheetByName(sheetName).appendRow(lastRowValues[0]);
14.      }
15.    }
16. }
```

This next part will get the sheets on the spreadsheet, then loop through them and if it finds a match to the student in the latest submission, it will get the submission and append it to that sheet.

Line 9: Get all the sheets and store them in the array *sheets*.

Line 10: Set up the **for loop** to loop through the sheets. We start at 0 and continue for the length of the array *sheets*.

Line 11: Each loop, we get the sheet name.

Line 12: Then, we just check if the name from the latest assignment (*lastRowValues[0][1]*) is the same as the sheet name.

Line 13: If it is, we get that sheet by its name and append the content of the latest form submission to it.

This is better than hard coding the name checks, check if sheetName === "Paul", etc, as this will work regardless of the names of sheets and the number of sheets.

If you want to share the sheet with each of your students but you don't want to share the other students' info, you could set up individual files for them and send the form responses into them, by getting their file, the sheet and setting the range with the response data.

Alternatively, without code you could use the **importrange** function in their individual files, to import the data from their sheets automatically into their file.

Example 3 - Appointment System

In this final example, we'll create a simple appointment system, where the user selects a time on the Google Form and submits it. The form is then updated, so when the next person opens it, the times previously selected don't appear, so aren't available. This will show how we can get the latest form responses from the form and then update the form based on that submission.

Here's the form:

5-AppointmentTimes

Form description

Name

Short answer text

Choose an appointment time *

○ 09:00

○ 09:30

○ 10:30

○ 11:00

○ 11:30

○ 12:00

We are just getting two pieces of information, their name and the appointment time.

The Code

Enter the following code in the <u>form</u> script editor.

```
1. function meetingTimes() {
2.    const form = FormApp.getActiveForm();
```

Lines 1-2: Set up the function and get the active form.

```
4. //Get current times on Form
5.    let timesArray = [];
6.    const cuestions = form.getItems();
7.    const timeQ = questions[1].asMultipleChoiceItem();
8.    const choices = timeQ.getChoices();
9.    for (var i = 0; i < choices.length; i++) {
10.       timesArray.push(choices[i].getValue());
11.    }
```

Line 5: Set up an empty array called *timesArray*. This is where we will put the appointment times.

Line 6: We get the questions from the form using **getItems()**.

Line 7: Get the question which contains the appointment time, i.e. *question[1]* (2nd question) and we get it as a multiple-choice item.

Line 8: We need to get the choices linked to that question, by using **getChoices()**.

Line 9: Now, we loop through all the choices (from 0 to the number of choices, i.e. the length of the array *choices*).

Line 10: Each loop, we get the value of the choice (i.e. what it says), and add it to the *timesArray* array, by using the **push** method.

```
[09:00, 09:30, 10:00, 10:30, 11:00, 11:30, 12:00]
```

As we can see, in *timesArray* above we have all the times. Now, we need to get the latest form submission and the time submitted. Lines 13-20, we've seen before in the form example above.

```
13.    //Get all form responses and the latest one
14.    const formResponses = form.getResponses(),
15.     latestFR = formResponses[form.getResponses().length-1];
```

Line 14: First, we get all the responses on the form.

Line 15: Then, we get the latest response by getting the last response in *formResponses*.

```
17.    //Get submitted time from form
18.    const itemResponses = latestFR.getItemResponses(),
19.     itemResponse = itemResponses[1],
20.     submittedTime = itemResponse.getResponse();
```

Line 18: Now, we need to get the specific response, which has the submitted time. We get the item responses from the latest form response.

Line 19: Then, we get the second item response, which is the time.

Line 20: Finally, we get the response of that specific item, i.e. the actual time. We place it in the variable *submittedTime*.

Now, we need to loop through *timesArray* and match the submitted time with one of the times in the array. Once found, we get the position of it, then remove it from the array.

```
22.     //Remove submittedTime from array
23.       for (x in timesArray){
24.         if(timesArray[x] === submittedTime) {
25.           const indexT = timesArray.indexOf(submittedTime);
26.           timesArray.splice(indexT, 1);
27.         }
28.       }
```

Line 23: This time will use the **for in** loop to go through all the items in the *timesArray* array.

Line 24: Each loop will check to see if the time in the array (at position x) is equal to the one submitted.

Line 25: If so, it will get the position of the time in the array by using the **indexOf()** method. This will return a number related to the array position.

Line 26: We can then use that number to remove the item from the array at that position by using the **splice()** method. This will get the item at that index and will remove one item from the *timesArray* array.

[09:00, 09:30, 10:30, 11:00, 11:30, 12:00]

As we can see it's removed the "10:00" option as that was the last one submitted by the user.

```
30.     //Replace time question on form with array
31.       timeQ.setChoiceValues(timesArray);
32.     }
```

Line 31: The final part is to update the form, so others can't select the same time. As we previously accessed the form and got the question with the times, we can use the same variable *timeQ* and we just need to set the choices using the *timesArray* array.

To make it work automatically on a form submission, we'll need to set up the trigger within the form as we saw earlier.

meetingTimes

Choose which deployment should run

Head

Select event source

From form

Select event type

On form submit

As we can see, if we open the form again, it has removed the 10:00 option.

Choose an appointment time *

○ 09:00

○ 09:30

○ 10:30

○ 11:00

○ 11:30

○ 12:00

If you want to re-set up the form with the times again, here's a little piece of code to do that, so you don't have to retype them in!

```
1. function setUpForm() {
2.   const form = FormApp.getActiveForm(),
3.     questions = form.getItems(),
4.     timeQ = questions[1].asMultipleChoiceItem();
5.
  timeQ.setChoiceValues(['09:00','09:30','10:00','10:30','11:00','11:30','12:00']);
6. }
```

Note, there is one potential problem and that is if more than one person has opened the form at the same time, the form won't update while it's open, so there is the potential that two people could choose the same time.

Hopefully, you can see that with very little code, you can do some really useful things with form responses.

You can find the full pieces of code for this chapter in Appendix 2.

CHAPTER 15: Form validation

In this chapter, we're going to look at automatically setting up validation on a form. Validation allows us to control what the user inputs on the form, for example, to make sure they enter a number, make sure they write more than 10 words, etc.

Clocking in & out form

In the example below, we're going to set up a simple clocking in and out form, which will require the employee to enter a 4-digit code. It will then add validation to the form to check that the code is valid. We'll also make the questions required to make the user have to fill them out before submitting the form. Here's the form:

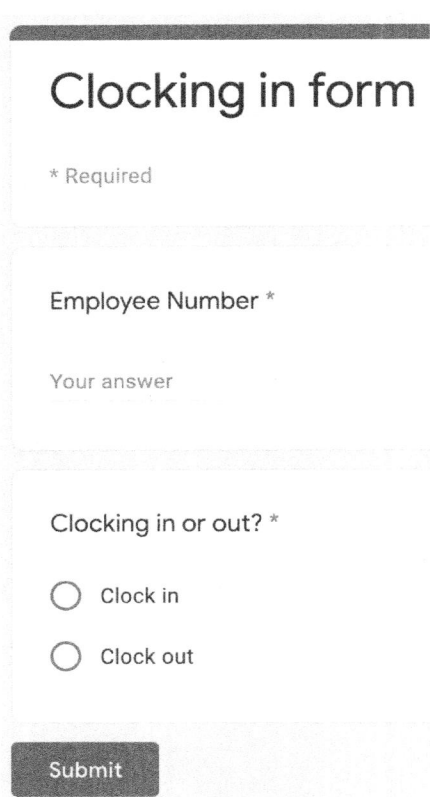

The Code

Either in a Google Sheet or Google Form, write the following code. We're going to create a new form, create the employee number question, then add validation to it.

```
1.  function setUpValidation() {
2.    //Set up form
3.    const form = FormApp.create('Clocking in');
4.    form.setTitle('Clocking in form');
```

Line 1: Set up the function.

Line 3: Create a new form using **FormApp.create()** and give it a name in the brackets.

Line 4: To give the form a title, get the form and set the title using **setTitle()**.

Now, let's add the employee number question.

```
6.    //Set up page
7.    const item = form.addTextItem()
8.                     .setTitle('Employee Number')
9.                     .setRequired(true);
```

Line 7: The question will require the employee to type in a number, so we need to add a text item. So, we get the form and use **addTextItem()**. Don't add a semi-colon on the end, as we going to add extra parts to this. Store this in the variable called *item*, as we will need to refer to this when we add the validation.

Line 8: Give the question a title, using **setTitle()**.

Line 9: Let's ensure the employee fills it out by using **setRequired()** and in the brackets stating true. This makes it a required question. Add the semi-colon on the end.

Now, let's add the validation to this question. The structure to this will be very similar for most types of validation. I.e. you create it, possibly set some help text, state the validation you want, then build it. At the end, you then need to set it to the question.

```
11.   const textVal = FormApp.createTextValidation()
12.      .setHelpText("Enter your 4 digit employee number.")
13.      .requireNumberEqualTo(1234)
14.      .build();
15.   item.setValidation(textVal);
```

Line 11: Create the validation and choose the appropriate one for your question type. As we're using a text item, we need to use **createTextValidation()**. Assign it to the variable *textVal*.

Line 12: We have the option of adding some help text, which will provide guidance to the user, as to what they need to enter. This is optional but is often a good idea. Use **setHelpText()** and write the help text in the brackets.

Line 13: Now, we add the validation we want. There are lots to choose from, but here we want the number typed in to be equal to their employee number, so we use **requireNumberEqualTo()** and in the brackets state the number it needs to equal.

Line 14: We then need to build our validation using **build()**, ending with a semi-colon.

Line 15: Finally, we need to add this validation to our question. We get the question, stored in the variable *item*, and use **setValidation()** and pass the variable *textVal*, which contains the validation, to it.

In the final part, we're going to set up a simple multiple-choice question, with two options, 'clock in' or 'clock out'.

```
17.     form.addMultipleChoiceItem()
18.         .setTitle('Clocking in or out?')
19.         .setChoiceValues(["Clock in", "Clock out"])
20.         .setRequired(true);
21.   }
```

Line 17: Add a multiple-choice item to the form. here there's no need to set up a variable as we're not going to work with the question later on.

Line 18: Set up the question title.

Line 19: Set the options of the question, using **setChoiceValues()** and state the options in the brackets, using an array.

Line 20: We'll also make this question a required one.

Line 21: Close the function.

Run the code (going through the usual authorization the first time) and you'll find the form created in your My Drive.

Clocking in

Open the form and you'll see the titles and questions that have been created.

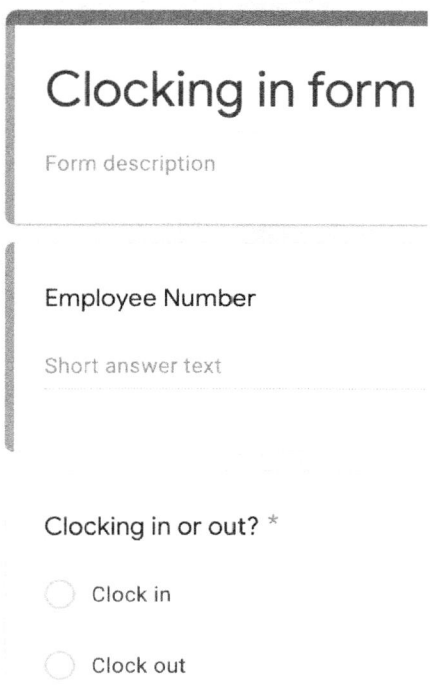

Clicking on the employee number question, we can see the validation has been set up, so that it checks to see if the number entered equals '1234'. Note, it ignores the decimal point.

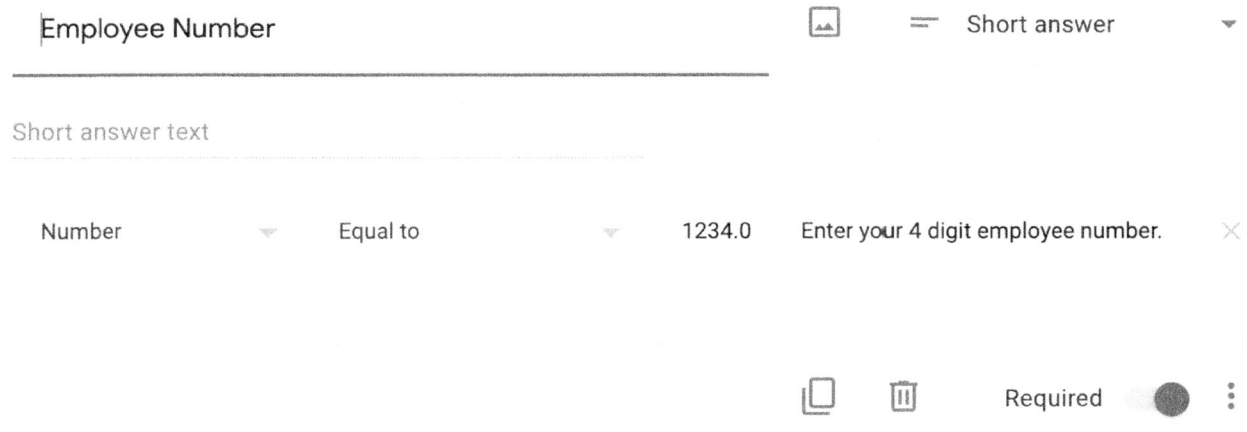

When the employee types in a number, if it's wrong, they see the help text that we set up.

Employee Number *

h
_____

⊘ Enter your 4 digit employee number.

Whereas, if they type in the correct number, the help text disappears.

Employee Number *

1234

Other validations

Here are the other validations you can set up:

Method
`requireNumber()`
`requireNumberBetween(start, end)`
`requireNumberEqualTo(number)`
`requireNumberGreaterThan(number)`
`requireNumberGreaterThanOrEqualTo(number)`
`requireNumberLessThan(number)`
`requireNumberLessThanOrEqualTo(number)`
`requireNumberNotBetween(start, end)`
`requireNumberNotEqualTo(number)`

```
requireTextContainsPattern(pattern)

requireTextDoesNotContainPattern(
  pattern)

requireTextDoesNotMatchPattern(
  pattern)

requireTextIsEmail()

requireTextIsUrl()

requireTextLengthGreaterThanOrEqualTo(
  number)

requireTextLengthLessThanOrEqualTo(
  number)

requireTextMatchesPattern(pattern)

requireWholeNumber()
```

You can find more information in the Google documentation here:

https://developers.google.com/apps-script/reference/forms/text-validation-builder

You can find the full piece of code for this chapter in Appendix 2.

CHAPTER 16: Form page navigation

In this chapter, we're going to expand on the previous chapter on setting up form validation and improve the clocking in and out form we set up, so that the same form can be used for different employees. We're going to use this example to see how page navigation can work, both to move to certain pages and to display the Submit button on a page.

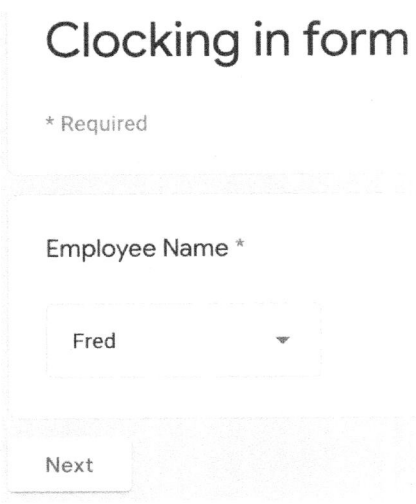

There will be 4 pages to our form and on the first page, we'll have a drop-down menu where the employee will choose their name and then click Next. This will then take them to their particular page in the form. Fred will go to page 2, Wilma to page 3, and Betty to page 4.

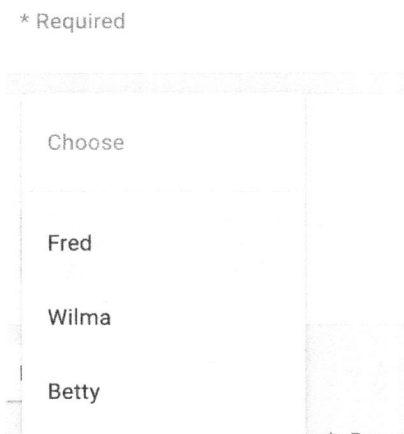

On their personal pages, the employees will have the same options. They will enter their employee number and they will state whether they are clocking in or out. Then, they will submit the form.

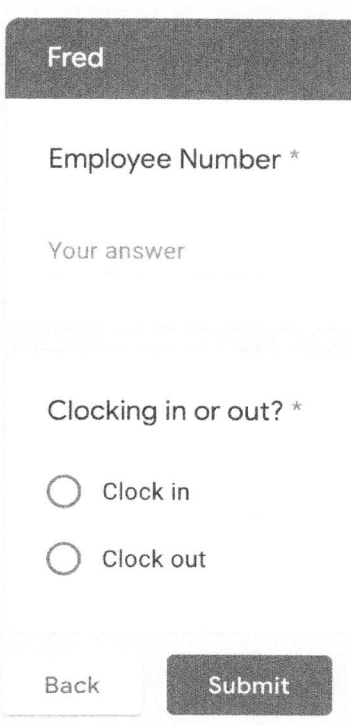

Some of the code below is similar to the chapter on Form Validation.

The Code

```
1.  function setUpForm() {
2.    //Set up form
3.    const form = FormApp.create('Clocking in v2');
4.    form.setTitle('Clocking in form');
```

Line 1: Set up the function.

Line 3: Create the new form.

Line 4: Add a title to the form using **setTitle()**.

Clocking in form - Page 1

On the first page, we're going to have a drop-down menu where the employee will select their name before clicking Next.

```
6.      //Set up first page
7.      const item1 = form.addListItem()
8.                      .setTitle('Employee Name')
9.                      .setRequired(true);
```

Line 7: We add the drop-down menu using **addListItem()**.

Line 8: Give the menu a title.

Line 9: Make it a required item using **setRequired()** and passing *true* in the brackets.

For now, we don't add the options, as we're going to need to state which pages those options will take us, and we need to set up the pages first.

```
11.     const page2 = form.addPageBreakItem()
12.                     .setTitle('Fred');
```

Line 11: Now, we add a page break at the end of page 1, using **addPageBreakItem()**. We add this to the variable *page2*, which we'll use later on to add the navigation to the different pages.

Line 12: We give the page break the title of the first employee on the list, 'Fred', even though this will actually appear on page **2**.

On pages 2, 3, and 4 we will have a question asking for their employee number and then a multiple-choice question asking if they are clocking in or out. The code for lines 14 to 28 is the same as we saw in the last chapter.

Clocking in form - Page 2

```
14.     //Set up second page (Fred)
15.     const item2 = form.addTextItem()
16.                     .setTitle('Employee Number')
17.                     .setRequired(true);
```

Line 15: Set up the first question, using **addTextItem()**. This question we'll assign to the variable *item2*.

Line 16: Give it a title.

Line 17: Make it a required question.

```
19.     const textVal2 = FormApp.createTextValidation()
20.         .setHelpText("Enter your 4 digit employee number.")
```

```
21.          .requireNumberEqualTo(1234)
22.          .build();
23.   item2.setValidation(textVal2);
```

Line 19: Now, we create the validation for the above question to check the number entered matches the number for that employee ('Fred').

Line 20: Set up the help text.

Line 21: Use the validation method **requireNumberEqualTo()** and add the number for that employee, in this case is '1234'.

Line 22: Build the validation.

Line 23: Add the validation to the question using **setValidation()** and add the validation *textVal2* in the brackets.

Now, we set up the clocking in or out question.

```
25.   form.addMultipleChoiceItem()
26.          .setTitle('Clocking in or out?')
27.          .setChoiceValues(["Clock in", "Clock out'])
28.          .setRequired(true);
```

Line 25: We create a multiple-choice question using **addMultipleChoiceItem()**.

Line 26: Give the question a title.

Line 27: Add the options to the question, putting the 2 options in the brackets as an array.

Line 28: Set the question as required.

At the end of this page, we want this employee, Fred, to then submit the form, we don't want him to click next and go to the following page, which will be Wilma's. So, we need to set up the **page navigation**.

```
30.   var page3 = form.addPageBreakItem()
31.              .setTitle('Wilma')
32.              .setGoToPage(FormApp.PageNavigationType.SUBMIT);
```

Line 30: We set up the page break as we did in line 11, just this time we'll assign it to the *page3* variable.

Line 31: Give it the next employee's name, 'Wilma'.

Line 32: Use the **setGoToPage()** method to set up the page navigation. Then in the brackets, state what type of page navigation you want. Here, we want a Submit button, so we use **FormApp.PageNavigationType.SUBMIT**.

Clocking in form - Page 3

We set up page 3 in the same way as page 2, except for the employee number for Wilma is different.

```
34.     //Set up third page (Wilma)
35.     const item3 = form.addTextItem()
36.                 .setTitle('Employee Number')
37.                 .setRequired(true);
38.
39.     const textVal3 = FormApp.createTextValidation()
40.         .setHelpText("Enter your 4 digit employee number.")
41.         .requireNumberEqualTo(3456)
42.         .build();
43.     item3.setValidation(textVal3);
44.
45.     form.addMultipleChoiceItem()
46.         .setTitle('Clocking in or out?')
47.         .setChoiceValues(["Clock in", "Clock out"])
48.         .setRequired(true);
49.
50.     const page4 = form.addPageBreakItem()
51.         .setTitle('Betty')
52.         .setGoToPage(FormApp.PageNavigationType.SUBMIT);
```

Clocking in form - Page 4

This is the same as pages 2 and 3 except that we don't need to add the page navigation at the end, as this page is the final page and the Submit button will appear automatically.

```
54.     //Set up forth page (Betty)
55.     const item4 = form.addTextItem()
56.                 .setTitle('Employee Number')
57.                 .setRequired(true);
58.
59.     const textVal4 = FormApp.createTextValidation()
60.         .setHelpText("Enter your 4 digit employee number.")
61.         .requireNumberEqualTo(6789)
62.         .build();
63.     item4.setValidation(textVal4);
64.     form.addMultipleChoiceItem()
```

```
65.        .setTitle('Clocking in or out?')
66.        .setChoiceValues(["Clock in", "Clock out"])
67.        .setRequired(true);
```

Now, we've set up the four pages, we need to go back and set up the options for the employee drop-down question on the first page.

```
70.     //Set up name choices on first page
71.     item1.setChoices([
72.       item1.createChoice("Fred", page2),
73.       item1.createChoice("Wilma", page3),
74.       item1.createChoice("Betty", page4)
75.     ]);
76.   }
```

Line 71: We get the question, stored in *item1*, and set up the options using **setChoices()**. We then add the options as array items.

Line 72: The first option, we set up by using **createChoice()**, then in the brackets add the text you want to show in the drop-down menu and then the page break item you want to navigate to. We stored the second page (Fred's) in the variable *page2* (see line 11).

Line 73: We do the same for the next page (Wilma's).

Line 74: And finally, for the last page (Betty's).

Lines 75-76: We close the array and the function.

Run the code and you'll see the new form in your My Drive.

 Clocking in v2

Opening the form, we can see it's set up the first page with the employee list question.

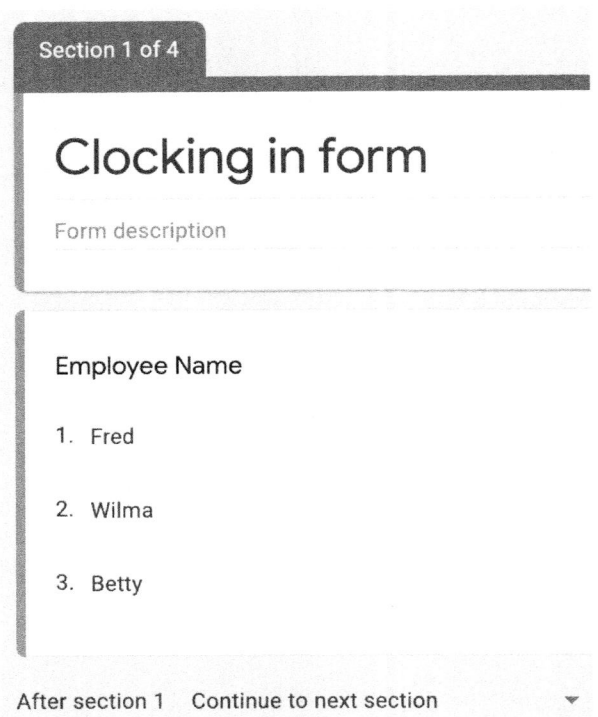

Clicking on the Employee Name question we can see it's set up the page navigation options for each name.

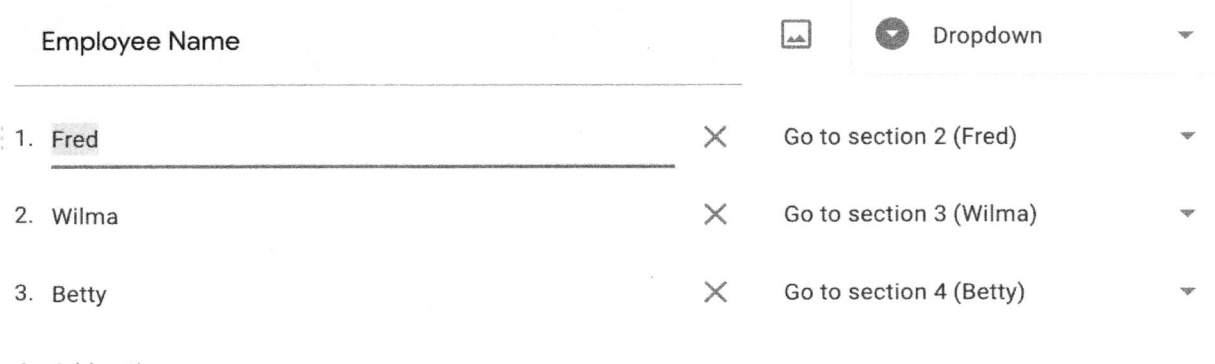

On the second page, we can see it's labelled it 'Fred' and set up the employee number and clocking in or out question.

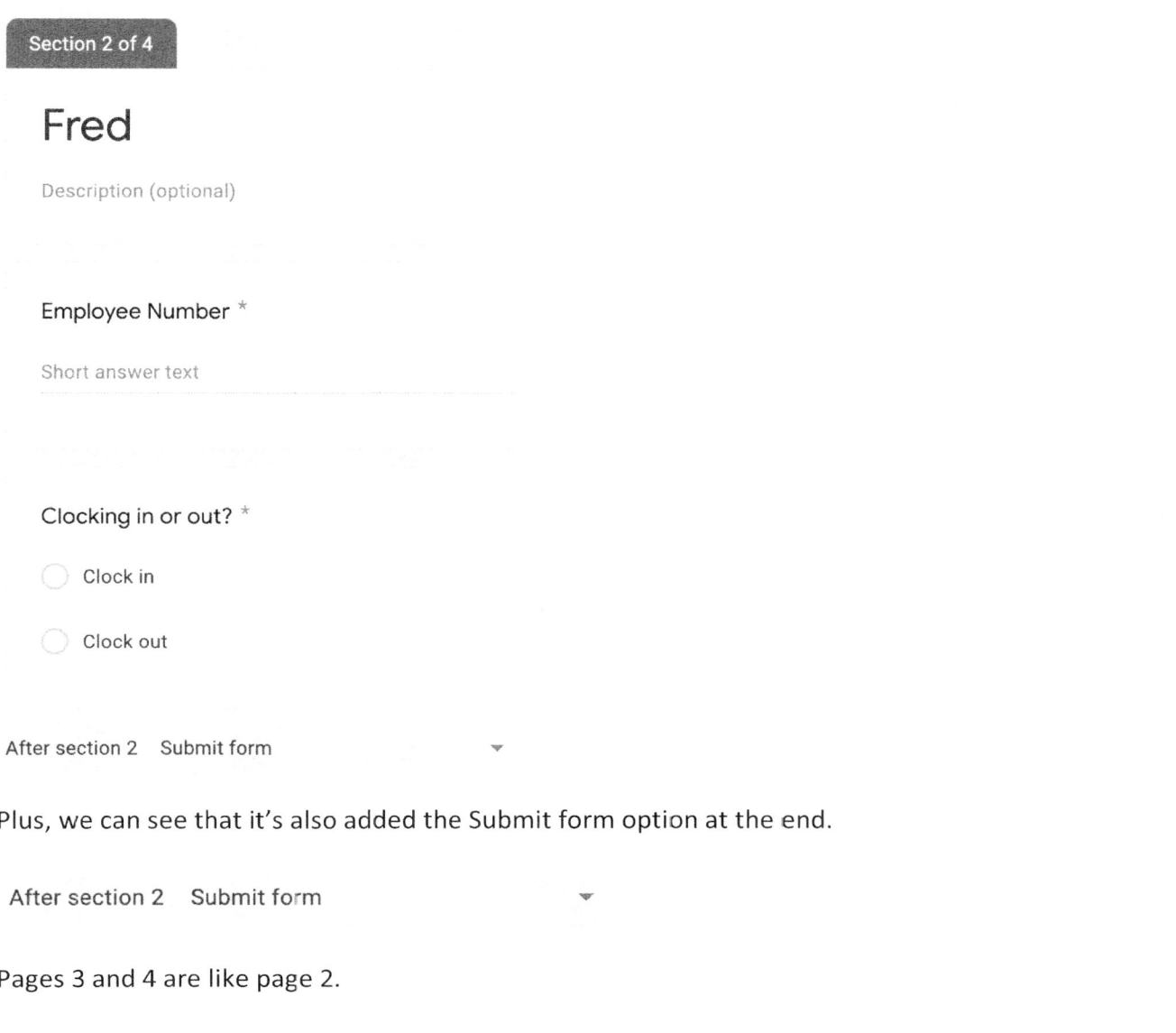

Plus, we can see that it's also added the Submit form option at the end.

After section 2   Submit form   ▼

Pages 3 and 4 are like page 2.

Opening the form view we can see the first page asks for the emplcyee's name via a drop-down menu.

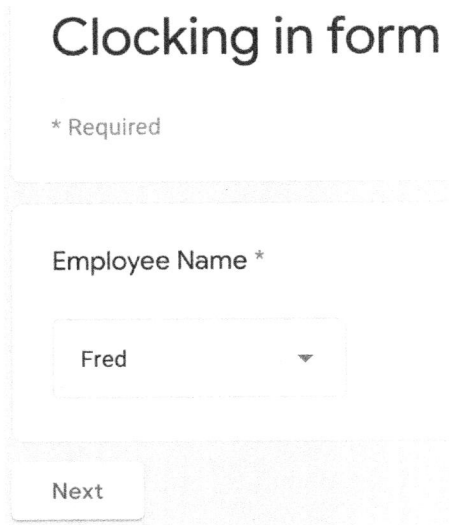

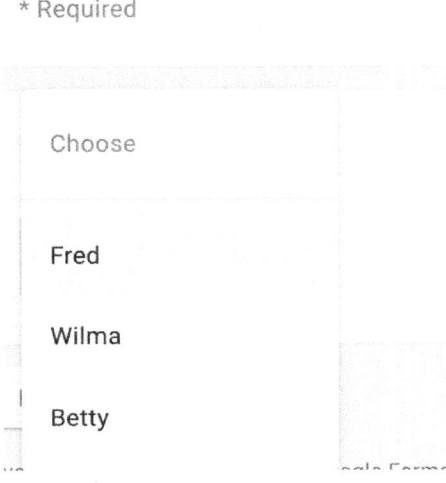

If we choose an employee, we can see it takes us to their page, where they will have to enter their employee number and clock in or out, then press Submit.

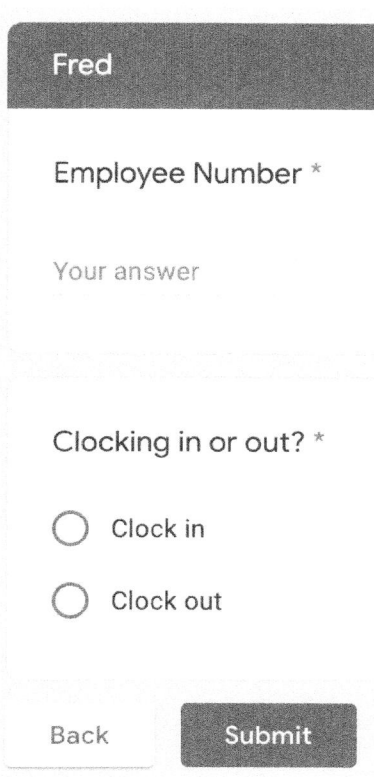

You can find the full piece of code for this chapter in Appendix 2.

CHAPTER 17: Making quizzes in Forms

In this chapter, we're going to look at how you can set up a **Google Forms quiz** with Apps Script. As an example, I'm going to take you through the example that was posted on the Google Cloud blog here:

https://cloud.google.com/blog/products/application-development/create-quizzes-in-google-forms-with

I've tweaked it a little just to create a new form instead of editing an existing one.

We're going to set up a simple one checkbox question quiz, which will contain the points for a correct answer and will then give the user feedback on their answer. If the answer is correct, they can see confirmation of this, and if it's wrong they will get a link to a Wikipedia page helping them get the question right.

As you'll see, it's really easy to set up and could then be easily adapted for other quizzes.

The Code

Instead of writing the code in the Script editor connected to a form or a sheet, we're going to create a standalone script in our Drive. In Drive, click on New.

Then select More > Google Apps Script.

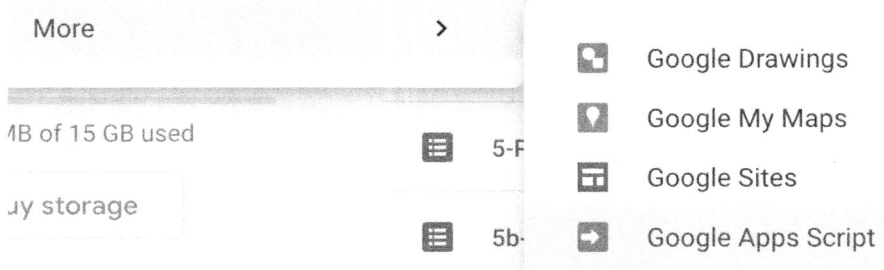

This will create a script project in you're my Drive and will open the script editor.

Alternatively, you can just type **script.new** in the Chrome address bar and this will also create a script project in you're my Drive.

```
1.  function createGradedCheckboxQuestionWithAutofeedback() {
2.    // Make sure the form is a quiz.
3.    const form = FormApp.create("Quiz");
4.    form.setIsQuiz(true);
```

First, let's create a new form.

Line 1: Set up the function.

Line 3: Create the new form and call it "Quiz".

Line 4: We then need to set the form up as a quiz using the **setIsQuiz()** method and stating *true* in the brackets.

Now, let's set up the question.

```
6.    // Make a 10 point question and set up the question
7.    const item = form.addCheckboxItem();
8.    item.setTitle("What flavors are in neapolitan ice cream?");
9.    item.setPoints(10);
```

Line 7: Add the checkbox question using **addCheckboxItem()** and store it in *item*.

Line 8: Give the question a title.

Line 9: Set the points value you want the question to have. Here, it's going to be a 10 pointer.

Now, create the choices for the questions and state which ones are correct and which are incorrect.

```
11.   // chocolate, vanilla, & strawberry are the correct answers
12.   item.setChoices([
13.     item.createChoice("chocolate", true),
14.     item.createChoice("vanilla", true),
15.     item.createChoice("rum raisin", false),
16.     item.createChoice("strawberry", true),
17.     item.createChoice("mint", false)
18.   ]);
```

Line 12: Set up the choices with **setChoices** and in the brackets, use the square brackets, as we've got an array of items for this question.

Line 13: We use **createChoice()** for each option and it carries 2 arguments: Option text and a boolean, *true* or *false*. 'true' means the option is a correct one and 'false' if it is incorrect. End the line with a comma as it's connecting it to the next line.

Note, in this example, to get the question correct, all the correct options need to be selected.

Lines 14-17: Repeat the same for each option. Don't add a comma after the last option.

Line 18: Close the array and brackets.

Now, we need to give some feedback to the user if the answer is correct or incorrect.

```
20.     // If the respondent answers correctly,
21.     // they'll see this feedback when they viewscores.
22.     const correctFeedback = FormApp.createFeedback()
23.         .setText("You're an ice cream expert!")
24.         .build();
25.     item.setFeedbackForCorrect(correctFeedback);
```

Line 22: First, we create the feedback using **createFeedback()**. Then we chain a couple of methods to it.

Line 23: First, we state what text we want to show in the feedback, using **setText()**.

Line 24: Then we 'build' the feedback.

Line 25: Finally, we need to set the feedback we've just built to the correct feedback. Just pass the variable *correctFeedback* inside the brackets.

We then go through a similar process for an incorrect answer. But this time we're going to give the user some help and add a link to page where they can find out more information about the ice-cream.

```
27.     // If they respond incorrectly, they'll see this feedback with
28.     // helpful link to read more about ice cream.
29.     const incorrectFeedback = FormApp.createFeedback()
30.         .setText("Sorry, wrong answer")
31.         .addLink(
32.             "https://en.wikipedia.org/wiki/Neapolitan_ice_cream",
33.     "Read more")
34.         .build();
35.     item.setFeedbackForIncorrect(incorrectFeedback);
36.     }
```

Line 29: Set up the feedback as before, this time we'll store it in the variable *incorrectFeedback*.

Line 30: Set the feedback text.

Lines 31-33: We use **addLink()** to add a link in the feedback. In the brackets, there are 2 arguments. One is the URL in speech marks. And secondly, the link text we want to show in the feedback message, rather than an ugly, long URL.

Line 34: Build the feedback.

Lines 35-36: Set it for the incorrect feedback, then close the function.

Run the code and authorize it.

The new form will appear in your My Drive.

Opening it, we can see that it has added the question, added the points, selected which questions are correct. Click on "Answer key".

Ice Cream Quiz

Form description

What flavors are in neapolitan ice cream?   Checkboxes

☐ chocolate   ✓   ✗
☐ vanilla   ✓   ✗
☐ rum raisin   ✗
☐ strawberry   ✓   ✗
☐ mint   ✗

☐ Add option or add "Other"

Answer key (10 points)   Required

Here we can see the points score and feedback messages for a correct or incorrect answer.

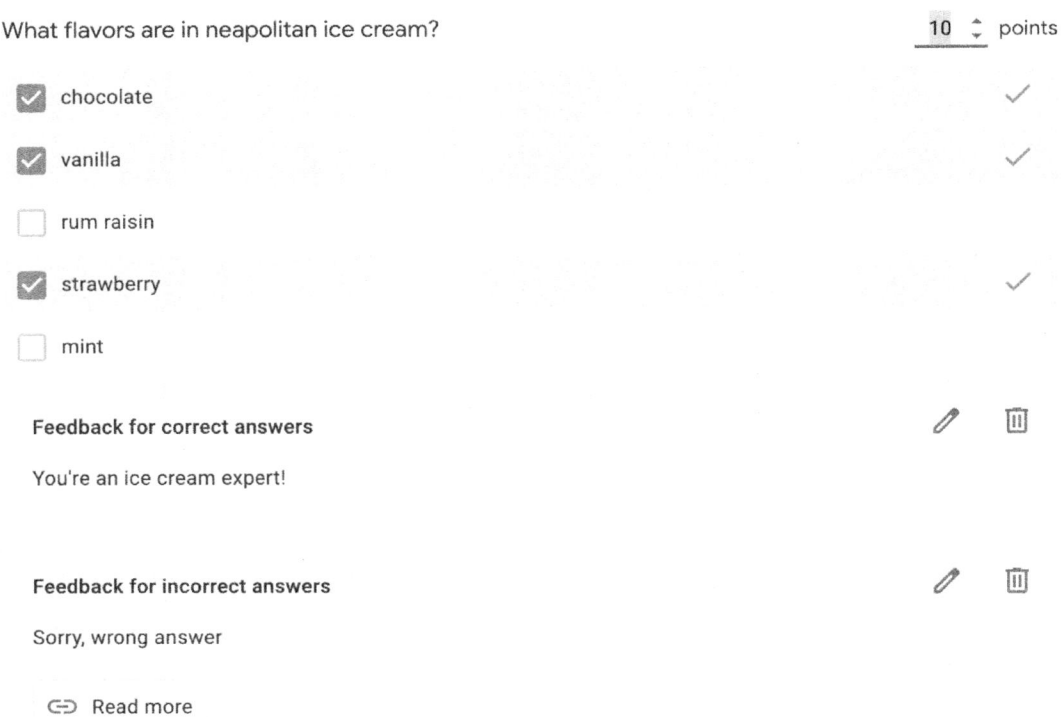

I want the user to be able to see the feedback as soon as they have submitted the form, so I need to select the option to release the mark immediately. You could also, add an email question and then select the option for them to receive the mark and feedback in an email.

Click on the Settings cog.

Then click on Quizzes.

Settings

General   Presentation   Quizzes

● **Make this a quiz**
Assign point values to questions and allow auto-grading.

Quiz options

Release grade:

○ Immediately after each submission

◉ Later, after manual review
Turns on email collection

Select "Immediately after each submission".

Release grade:

◉ Immediately after each submission

Then click Save.

Click on the eye icon to open the form in the user view. All the user will see is the question and the 5 options.

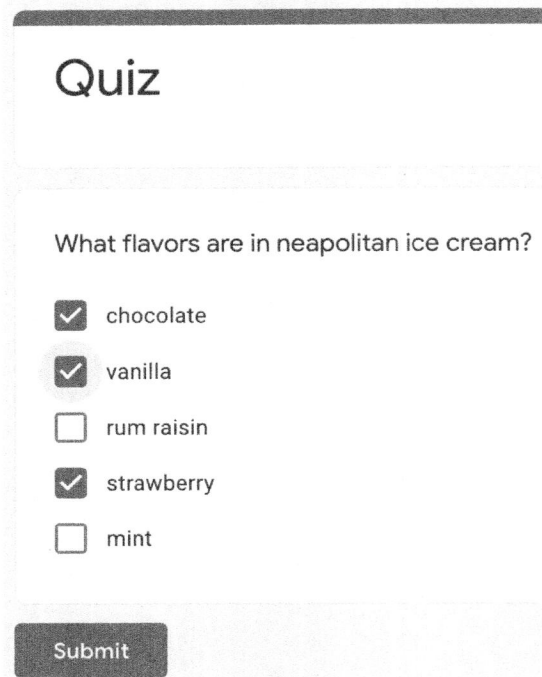

If we tick the correct ones and submit the form, we'll see the confirmation message. Then click "View your accuracy".

Quiz

Your response has been recorded.

[View accuracy]

Submit another response

As we can see, it's shows the answers I chose and gives the correct feedback.

Quiz

What flavors are in neapolitan ice cream?

- ☑ chocolate
- ☑ vanilla
- ☐ rum raisin
- ☑ strawberry
- ☐ mint

Feedback

You're an ice cream expert!

If I answered the question incorrectly, when I click on "View your accuracy" I receive the incorrect feedback and I can see the link that was set up earlier.

Quiz

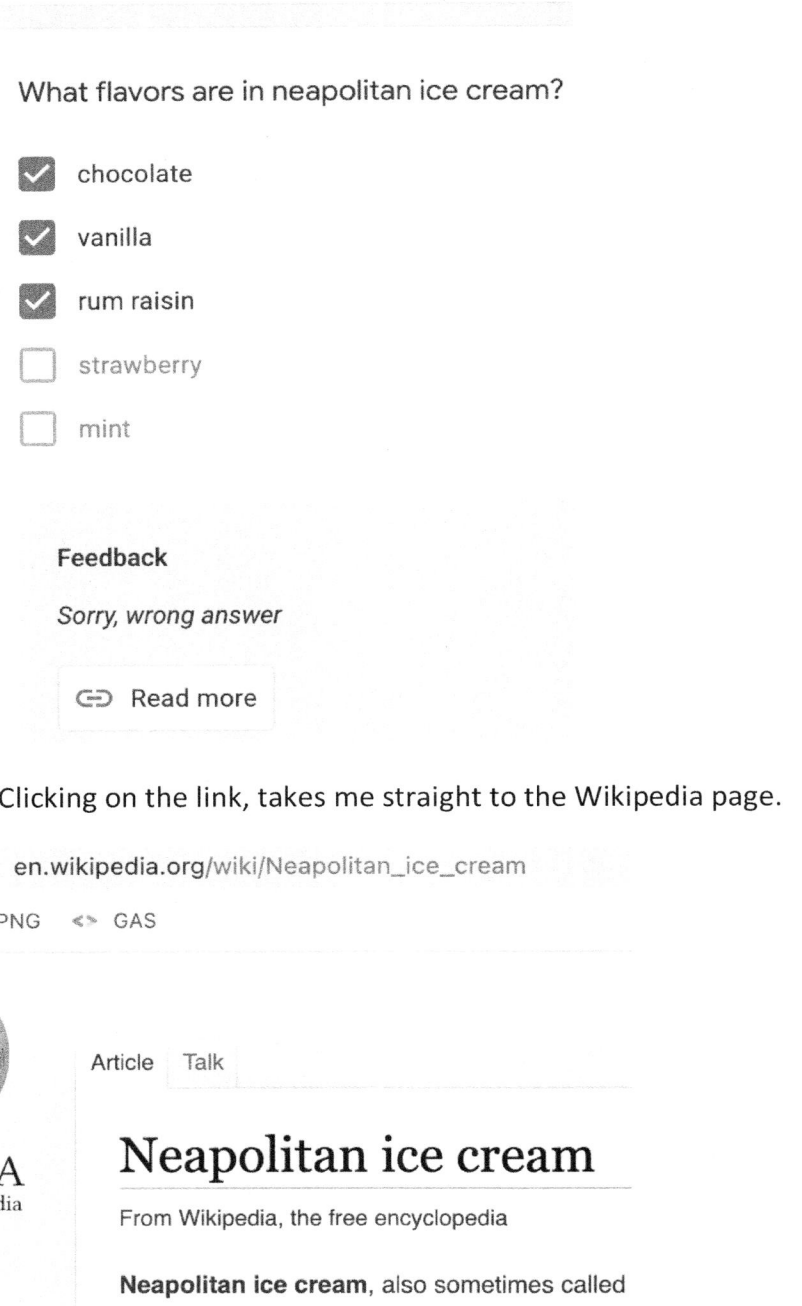

Clicking on the link, takes me straight to the Wikipedia page.

en.wikipedia.org/wiki/Neapolitan_ice_cream

PNG   <> GAS

You can find all the code for this chapter in Appendix 2.

Further Reading

Other Apps Script books by this author available on Amazon:

Beginner's Guide to Google Apps Script 3 – Drive 	<ul><li>This book goes through using Apps Script with Google Drive.</li><li>It covers:</li><li>Creating files and folders in My Drive and in a specific folder</li><li>Making copies of files</li><li>Creating folders from a URL</li><li>Moving files and folders and adding shortcuts</li><li>Adding and removing editors</li><li>Copying a Google and making a PDF from it</li><li>Getting contents of a Drive folder</li><li>Getting files by type</li><li>Creating download URLs</li><li>Automatically send a brochure when a Form is submitted</li><li>Searching for files and folders</li></ul>

Step-by-step Guide to Google Apps Script 4 – Documents 	<ul><li>This book goes through using Apps Script with Google Docs</li><li>It covers:</li><li>Creating a Google Doc from a form submission</li><li>Master Document copier</li><li>Edit a document template using placeholders</li><li>Making an invoice with multiple items</li><li>Making a document from scratch</li><li>Making student reports with progress bars</li><li>Emailing reports as a PDF or as a link</li><li>Creating multiple reports in one document</li><li>Emailing specific conference information</li><li>Sending conference info via a web app</li><li>Update document from data on the web</li></ul>
Google Apps Script Projects 1 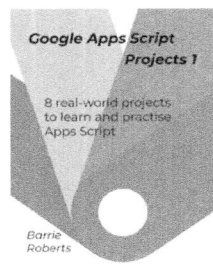	<ul><li>This book goes through 8 real-world practical projects step-by-step to help you practise your Apps Script skills.</li><li>Projects: -Book inventory -Make sheets and documents per student -Placement test -Copy folder content -Set up new employee -Issues reporting with translation -Multiple files and folder maker -Send certificates to students</li></ul>

Other books and ebooks available by this author on Amazon:

Beginner's Guide to Google Drive	Beginner's Guide to Google Sheets	Beginner's Guide to Google Docs	Google Sheet Functions – A step-by-step guide
Step-by-step guide to Google Forms	Step-by-step guide to Google Sites	Step-by-step guide to Google Slides	Step-by-step guide to Google Meet

Here are some places I recommend you check out to learn even more about Apps Script.

Apps Script Websites

GOOGLE APPS SCRIPT

 Google Apps Script

https://developers.google.com/apps-script/reference

This is Google's official Apps Script site, which contains lists of Apps Script code that you'll need for your programs. In a lot of cases, it'll give you example chunks which you can copy and paste right into your program. Bookmark it, you'll be using it a lot!

STACK OVERFLOW

stackoverflow.com

Got stuck? Need someone to help you with your code. This is an amazing place where you can either search for an answer to your coding problem or post a question and the community invariably will post potential solutions.

W3SCHOOLS

w3schools.com

http://www.w3schools.com/js/

I've made reference to this site throughout this book. The W3Schools site covers all sorts of programming languages, but I highly recommend taking the time to read through the JavaScript entries and try out the challenges it sets, to get a good idea of how it works. It's then useful in the future as a reference, as most parts contain example code so you know how to use it.

DESKTOP LIBERATION - BRUCE MCPHERSON

Desktop Liberation

http://ramblings.mcpher.com/Home/excelquirks/gassnips

The man is a font of knowledge, and his blog contains a stack of GAS examples, which include the code so you see how he goes about it.

CODEACADEMY

https://www.codecademy.com/learn/learn-javascript

This site allows you to learn various programming languages by doing. Each part there is a challenge where you have to write or edit code, to be able to pass on to the next section. Bit by bit this builds up your JavaScript knowledge.

APPS SCRIPT BOOKS

Google Apps Script for Beginners – Serge Gabet

This starts from the basics and covers various uses of GAS, including with Sheets, Forms, Emails, Docs, and some web applications improving the UI.

Learning Google Apps Script – Ramalingam Ganapathy

Personally, I think this is a better book than the GAS for beginners and it takes you further. It covers areas like creating elements, emails, forms, calendar, RSS feeds, workflows, Add-ons. Here you'll see how the various parts of GAS come together to produce programs that carry out a complete workflow.

Going GAS – Bruce McPherson

It's full of great examples of GAS code, which you can use and experiment with. The idea of the book is for those coming from a VBA background, but I don't think that does the book justice, as I don't know anything about VBA and have still found this a very useful book. I've since gone back and reread it and it continues to be a great help.

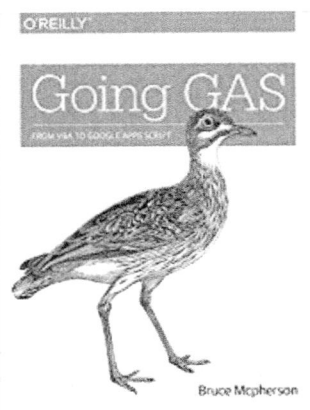

APPS SCRIPT VIDEOS

There is very limited training material out there in video format but here are three that I would recommend.

Apps Script Blastoff! - Ben Collins

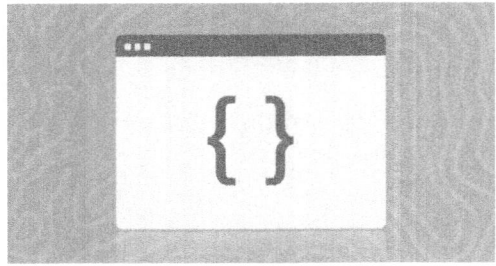

This is a free course from Ben Collins who produces some excellent Google Sheet and Apps Script video courses. I would definitely recommend signing up as it would complement this course well and also includes key JavaScript areas.

https://courses.benlcollins.com/p/apps-script-blastoff/?affcode=69396_kqpndtf0

Automation with Apps Script – Ben Collins

This course is more advanced and takes you further than the content of this book. Highly recommended. Note, Ben only runs this course periodically, but there is a waiting list you can sign up to.

https://courses.benlcollins.com/a/aff_nhd9f94m/external?affcode=69396_kqpndtf0

GOOGLE APPS SCRIPT GOOGLE GROUP COMMUNITY

This community is full of wonderful people willing to share ideas and to help you if you get stuck. It's growing all the time and just shows how popular Apps Script is becoming.

https://groups.google.com/forum/#!forum/google-apps-script-community

About the author

I'm one of the Tech coordinator at a language academy in Seville, Spain. I started off my career as a Quality Engineer in the automotive industry, then in the white goods industry and during that time I saw a wide range of companies and industries. If Google Apps Script and Google Workspace had existed then, it would have revolutionized the way we would have worked, in particular, automating and simplifying our admin processes.

I started using Google Apps and Drive around 2013 and quickly saw what a wonderful range of products they are and they have transformed the way we work at our academy. In 2015, I came across Google Apps Script, which I hadn't realized had been sitting hidden behind some of the Google Workspace products all the time! Looking back, it seems a natural progression from getting more into Google Sheets, learning more about the functions that are available and that can both simplify working with data and also provide insights not previously explored. Apps Script seemed to be the way to extend this functionality even further.

At first, I didn't really know what Apps Script could do and what I was going to use it for. I tried a couple of the examples on the Apps Script site and was amazed that for example, just by filling in a form, Apps Script could send confirmation emails, add an event to a person's calendar, and record how many people were going to the event.

I didn't just start learning Apps Script on its own. I knew it was built around JavaScript and so I spent time learning that, but what I did notice was that most of the books and websites out there only talk about its use with website design. I was also interested in this, so I also learnt HTML, CSS and JQuery. These aren't essential to learn if you're just starting out to use Apps Script, but when you start using it more, you realize that you can incorporate these into your code allowing you to produce professional looking web apps. This of course, is beyond the scope of a beginner's book but hopefully you can see that Apps Script can link with all of these and what you've learnt in this book is just the tip of the iceberg.

Now, we use Apps Script throughout department, automating tasks and allowing to do things that weren't possible before. For example, we have:

- An appointment system for parents to arrange meetings with the teachers;

- An attendance system with teachers using Google Forms on their phones and the data stored and stats produced automatically in Google Sheets;
- A book inventory web app to control the location of books;
- Reports to parents and companies – Using a combination of Google Sheets and Docs and then emailing the reports directly to parents and companies;
- Setting up monthly documents – automating this laborious and boring task;
- Auto emailing a specific team when class requests are filled out on a Google Form
- An Issues log to report problems, which incidentally is multi-lingual and Apps script does the translation for us.

This has allowed us to remove, simplify, and automate admin procedures, which in turn, has allowed us to spend more time with our customers and has allowed us to improve our services.

So, yes, I do think Apps Script is great! It's a great place to start if you're new to coding and if you want to get the most out of the Google workspace products and services.

If you have any questions about the scripts in this book, then please contact me at baz@bazroberts.com

Finally, I big thank you for purchasing this book. I really do hope this book gives you a good solid base to allow you to create some great programs.

Barrie "Baz" Roberts

Revision 10 - January 2022

FEEDBACK

I would love to hear your thoughts on this book! It would be great, if you could spare a minute to fill in this short feedback form:

bit.ly/BazsBooks

WEBSITE AND TWITTER

I post and share blog posts and information related to Google Apps Script and Google Workspace on my website www.bazroberts.com and on Twitter: **@barrielroberts**

Appendix 1 – Files and Code from each chapter

Chapter 1 – First Script

File: http://bit.ly/3vxruRy

```
1. function myFunction() {
2. SpreadsheetApp.getActiveSpreadsheet().getActiveSheet().getRange("A1").setValue('Hello!');
3. }
```

Chapter 2 – Variables and Getting & Setting Values

File: http://bit.ly/38PvT8O

```
1.  function collateMarks() {
2.    const ss = SpreadsheetApp.getActiveSpreadsheet();
3.    const sheet = ss.getActiveSheet();
4.
5.    sheet.getRange("A1").setValue("Name");
6.    sheet.getRange("B1").setValue("Subject");
7.    sheet.getRange("C1").setValue("Mark");
8.
9.    const student1 = sheet.getRange("F2:H2").getValues();
10.    const student2 = sheet.getRange("F5:H5").getValues();
11.    const student3 = sheet.getRange("F8:H8").getValues();
12.
13.    sheet.getRange("A2:C2").setValues(student1);
14.    sheet.getRange("A3:C3").setValues(student2);
15.    sheet.getRange("A4:C4").setValues(student3);
16.
17.    const header = sheet.getRange("A1:C1");
18.    header.setBackground("yellow")
19.        .setFontWeight("bold");
20.
21.    const table = sheet.getRange("A1:C4");
22.    table.setHorizontalAlignment("center");
23.  }
```

Chapter 3 – Loops

File: http://bit.ly/3ePC7JI

```
1.  //Print Hello!" 20 times down column A
2.  function loop1() {
3.    const ss = SpreadsheetApp.getActiveSpreadsheet().getSheetByName("Numbers");
4.
5.    for (r=1; r<21; r+=1) {
6.      ss.getRange(r,1).setValue("Hello!");
7.    }
8.  }
9.
10. //Print numbers 1 to 20 down column A
11. function loop2() {
12.   const ss = SpreadsheetApp.getActiveSpreadsheet().getSheetByName("Numbers");
13.
14.   for (r=1; r<21; r++) {
15.     ss.getRange(r,1).setValue(r);
16.   }
17. }
18.
19. //Fill cells A1 to A20 in blue
20. function loop3() {
21.   const ss = SpreadsheetApp.getActiveSpreadsheet().getSheetByName("Numbers");
22.
23.   for (r=1; r<21; r++) {
24.     ss.getRange(r,1).setBackground("blue");
25.   }
26. }
27.
28. //Fill cells A1 to A20 in blue and print numbers 1 to 20
29. function loop4() {
30.   const ss = SpreadsheetApp.getActiveSpreadsheet().getSheetByName("Numbers");
31.
32.   for (r=1; r<21; r++) {
33.     ss.getRange(r,1).setBackground("blue")
34.                     .setValue(r);
35.   }
36. }
37.
38. //Print 10 columns of numbers 1 to 20
39. function loop5() {
40.   const ss = SpreadsheetApp.getActiveSpreadsheet().getSheetByName("Numbers");
41.
42.   for (c=1; c<11; c++) {
43.
44.     for (r=1; r<21; r++) {
45.       ss.getRange(r,c).setValue(r);
46.     }
```

```
47.   }
48. }
49.
50. //Create 5 documents naming them Document1 to Document5
51. function loop6() {
52.   const ss = SpreadsheetApp.getActiveSpreadsheet().getSheetByName("Numbers");
53.
54.   for (r=1; r<6; r++) {
55.     DocumentApp.create("Document"+r);
56.   }
57. }
58.
59. //Create 4 documents each with student's name (use sheet called Names)
60. function loop7() {
61.   const ss = SpreadsheetApp.getActiveSpreadsheet().getSheetByName("Names");
62.
63.   for (r=1; r<5; r++) {
64.     let studentName = ss.getRange(r,1).getValue();
65.     DocumentApp.create("Document-"+studentName);
66.   }
67. }
68.
69.
70. function varLetDifference() {
71.   const ss = SpreadsheetApp.getActiveSpreadsheet().getSheetByName("Numbers");
72.
73.   for (r=1; r<21; r++) {
74.     ss.getRange(r,1).setValue(r);
75.     var v = r+1;
76.     let l = r+1;
77.   }
78.   Logger.log(v);
79.   Logger.log(l);
80. }
```

Chapter 4 – Arrays, Log & Executions

File: http://bit.ly/3bSeRbR

```
1. //Gets the numbers from the sheet and logs them in the log
2. function logNumbers(){
3.   const ss = SpreadsheetApp.getActiveSpreadsheet().getActiveSheet();
4.
5.   for (r=1; r<21; r++) {
6.     const listOfNumbers = ss.getRange(r,1).getValue();
7.
8.     Logger.log(listOfNumbers);
9.   }
```

```
10.  }
11.
12.  //Show a variable with 1 item and a variable with an array of items
13.  function array1a(){
14.    const ss = SpreadsheetApp.getActiveSpreadsheet().getActiveSheet();
15.
16.    const item = "Fred";
17.    const items = ["Joan", "Paula", "Dingo", "Georgina"];
18.
19.    Logger.log(item);
20.    Logger.log(items);
21.  }
22.
23.  //Showing the difference between setting a single value and an array
24.  function array1b(){
25.    const ss = SpreadsheetApp.getActiveSpreadsheet().getActiveSheet();
26.
27.    const item = "Fred";
28.    const items = ["Joan", "Paula", "Dingo", "Georgina"];
29.
30.    ss.getRange("D1").setValue(item);
31.
32.    ss.getRange("E1").setValue(items);
33.
34.    ss.getRange("F1").setValue(items[1]);
35.  }
36.
37.  //Uses getValues to get an array of numbers in one go; How to add them to a sheet
38.  function array2(){
39.    const ss = SpreadsheetApp.getActiveSpreadsheet().getActiveSheet();
40.
41.    const listOfNumbers = ss.getRange("A1:A20").getValues();
42.
43.    Logger.log(listOfNumbers);
44.
45.    ss.getRange("H1:H20").setValues(listOfNumbers);
46.
47.    ss.getRange("I1").setValue(listOfNumbers[1]);
48.  }
49.
50.  //Showing how arrays relate to rows and columns
51.  function array3(){
52.    const ss = SpreadsheetApp.getActiveSpreadsheet().getActiveSheet();
53.    const oneRowOfItems = [["Joan", "Paula", "Dingo", "Georgina"]];
54.    const twoRowsOfItems = [["Wilma", "Fred", "Betty", "Barney"], [35, 45, 30, 40]];
55.    ss.getRange(3,4,1,4).setValues(oneRowOfItems);
56.    ss.getRange(5,4,2,4).setValues(twoRowsOfItems);
57.  }
58.
59.  //How to loop through an array
60.  function array4(){
61.    const ss = SpreadsheetApp.getActiveSpreadsheet().getActiveSheet();
62.    const items = ["Joan", "Paula", "Dingo", "Georgina"];
63.
64.    for (i=1; i<5; i++) {
65.      ss.getRange(i,11).setValue(items[i-1]);
```

```
66.    }
67.  }
68.
69.  //Getting values one by one from a sheet and one by one adding them to a sheet
70.  function array5a(){
71.    const ss = SpreadsheetApp.getActiveSpreadsheet().getActiveSheet();
72.    let listOfNames = [];
73.
74.    for (r=1; r<5; r++) {
75.
76.      let name = ss.getRange(r,11).getValue();
77.      listOfNames.push(name);
78.
79.      Logger.log(listOfNames);
80.
81.      ss.getRange("M"+r).setValue(listOfNames[r-1]);
82.    }
83.  }
84.
85.  //Getting a range of values in one go and adding them to a sheet in one go
86.  //Note the different in execution time between array5a and 5b
87.  function array5b(){
88.    const ss = SpreadsheetApp.getActiveSpreadsheet().getActiveSheet();
89.
90.    const originalList2 = ss.getRange(1,11,4).getValues();
91.
92.    Logger.log(originalList2);
93.
94.    ss.getRange(1,15,4).setValues(originalList2);
95.  }
```

Chapter 5 – If, Prompt, Menu & OnOpen Trigger

File: http://bit.ly/3bUmFKp

```
1.  function onOpen() {
2.    SpreadsheetApp.getUi()
3.      .createMenu('New menu')
4.      .addItem('Example 1', 'example1')
5.      .addItem('Example 2', 'example2')
6.      .addItem('Example 3', 'example3')
7.      .addItem('Example 4', 'example4')
8.      .addItem('Example 5', 'example5')
9.      .addItem('Example 6', 'example6')
10.       .addItem('Return to Sheet1', 'example6b')
11.       .addItem('Example 7', 'example7')
12.       .addItem('Example 8', 'example8')
13.       .addItem('Example 9', 'example9')
14.       .addToUi();
```

```
15. }

1.  //Set background to red if attendance is less than 80%
2.  function example1() {
3.    const ss = SpreadsheetApp.getActiveSheet();
4.    const cellB3 = ss.getRange("B3");
5.    const attendance = cellB3.getValue();
6.
7.    if (attendance < 0.8) {
8.      cellB3.setBackground("red");
9.    }
10. }
11.
12. //Set background to red if attendance is less than 80%
13. //Otherwise set it to green
14. function example2() {
15.   const ss = SpreadsheetApp.getActiveSheet();
16.   const cellB3 = ss.getRange("B3");
17.   const attendance = cellB3.getValue();
18.
19.   if (attendance < 0.8) {
20.     cellB3.setBackground("red");
21.   }
22.
23.   else {
24.     cellB3.setBackground("green");
25.   }
26. }
27.
28. //Set background to red if attendance is less than 70%
29. //Set background to yellow if attendance is 70-80%
30. //Set background to green if attendance is 80% or more
31. function example3() {
32.   const ss = SpreadsheetApp.getActiveSheet();
33.   const cellB3 = ss.getRange("B3");
34.   const attendance = cellB3.getValue();
35.
36.   if (attendance < 0.7) {
37.     cellB3.setBackground("red");
38.   }
39.
40.   else if (attendance < 0.8) {
41.     cellB3.setBackground("yellow");
42.   }
43.
44.   else {
45.     cellB3.setBackground("green");
46.   }
47. }
48.
49. //Set background of name to red if
50. //attendance is less than 80% OR exam is less than 70%
51. function example4() {
52.   const ss = SpreadsheetApp.getActiveSheet();
53.   const cellD3 = ss.getRange("D3");
54.   const attendance = ss.getRange("E3").getValue();
55.   const exam = ss.getRange("F3").getValue();
56.
```

```
57.       if (attendance < 0.8 || exam < 0.7) {
58.         cellD3.setBackground("red");
59.       }
60.
61.       else {
62.         cellD3.setBackground("green");
63.       }
64.   }
65.
66.   //Set background of name to green if
67.   //attendance is 80% or more AND exam is 70% or more
68.   function example5() {
69.       const ss = SpreadsheetApp.getActiveSheet();
70.       const cellD3 = ss.getRange("D3");
71.       const attendance = ss.getRange("E3").getValue();
72.       const exam = ss.getRange("F3").getValue();
73.
74.       if (attendance >= 0.8 && exam >= 0.7) {
75.         cellD3.setBackground("green");
76.       }
77.
78.       else {
79.         cellD3.setBackground("red");
80.       }
81.   }
82.
83.   //Open sheet from name in cell B5 and paste student's data
84.   function example6() {
85.       const ss = SpreadsheetApp.getActiveSpreadsheet();
86.       const sheet1 = ss.getSheetByName('Sheet1');
87.       const name = sheet1.getRange("B5").getValue();
88.
89.       if(name === "John") {
90.         var figures = sheet1.getRange("A7:E9").getValues();
91.       }
92.
93.       else if(name === "Ringo") {
94.         var figures = sheet1.getRange("A10:E12").getValues();
95.       }
96.
97.       else if(name === "Paul") {
98.         var figures = sheet1.getRange("A13:E15").getValues();
99.       }
100.
101.      else if(name === "George") {
102.        var figures = sheet1.getRange("A16:E18").getValues();
103.      }
104.
105.      const studentSheet = ss.getSheetByName(name).activate();
106.      studentSheet.getRange("A1:E3").setValues(figures);
107.  }
108.
109.  //Return back to Sheet1
110.  function example6b() {
111.      const ss = SpreadsheetApp.getActiveSpreadsheet();
112.      const sheet1 = ss.getSheetByName('Sheet1').activate();
113.  }
114.
```

```
115. //Ask which sheet user wants to open and then open it
116. function example7() {
117.    const ss = SpreadsheetApp.getActiveSpreadsheet();
118.    const ui = SpreadsheetApp.getUi();
119.    const response = ui.prompt('Enter name:');
120.
121.    if (response.getSelectedButton() === ui.Button.OK) {
122.       const name = response.getResponseText();
123.       ss.getSheetByName(name).activate();
124.    }
125. }
126.
127. //Using ternary operator-If less than 80% set background red, otherwise green
128. function example8() {
129.    const ss = SpreadsheetApp.getActiveSheet();
130.    const cellB3 = ss.getRange("B3");
131.    const attendance = cellB3.getValue();
132.    (attendance < 0.8) ? cellB3.setBackground("red"):cellB3.setBackground("green");
133. }
134.
135. //Set background colour for all students' attendance figures
136. function example9() {
137.    const ss = SpreadsheetApp.getActiveSpreadsheet();
138.    const sheet1 = ss.getSheetByName('Sheet1');
139.    const attendanceFigures = sheet1.getRange("I3:I6").getValues();
140.
141.    for (i=0;i<attendanceFigures.length;i++){
142.
143.       let r = i+3;
144.       let rangeToChangeColour = sheet1.getRange(r,9);
145.
146.       if (attendanceFigures[i] < 0.7) {
147.          rangeToChangeColour.setBackground("red");
148.       }
149.
150.       else if (attendanceFigures[i] < 0.8) {
151.          rangeToChangeColour.setBackground("yellow");
152.       }
153.
154.       else {
155.          rangeToChangeColour.setBackground("green');
156.       }
157.    }
158. }
```

Chapter 6 – SpreadsheetApp and for in loop

File: http://bit.ly/3cKSLaN

```
1.  //Create menu to run examples from
2.  function onOpen() {
3.    SpreadsheetApp.getUi()
4.      .createMenu("Examples")
5.      .addItem("example 1", "example1")
6.      .addItem("example 2", "example2")
7.      .addItem("example 3", "example3")
8.      .addItem("example 4", "example4")
9.      .addItem("example 5", "example5")
10.     .addItem("example 6", "example6")
11.     .addItem("example 7", "example7")
12.     .addToUi();
13. }
```

```
1.  //Global variables
2.  const SS = SpreadsheetApp.getActiveSpreadsheet();
3.  const SHEET = SS.getActiveSheet();
4.
5.  //Create a new spreadsheet
6.  function example1() {
7.    SpreadsheetApp.create("New Spreadsheet1");
8.  }
9.
10. //Create a new spreadsheet with 20 rows and 10 columns
11. function example2() {
12.   SpreadsheetApp.create("New Spreadsheet2", 20, 10);
13. }
14.
15. //Create a new spreadsheet with a name from a sheet
16. function example3() {
17.   const name = SHEET.getRange("A1").getValue();
18.   SpreadsheetApp.create(name);
19. }
20.
21. //Create multiple spreadsheets with different names from a sheet
22. function example4() {
23.   const names = SHEET.getRange("B1:B3").getValues();
24.   for (i in names) {
25.     SpreadsheetApp.create(names[i]);
26.   }
27. }
28.
29. //Get a value from one spreadsheet and add it into another, using its URL
30. function example5() {
31.   const text = SHEET.getRange("C1").getValue();
32.   const newSS = SpreadsheetApp.openByUrl("https://docs.google.com/spreadsheets/d/1xFwNEaBjvHeBfxW_z4wBsyozedn5sQ82FWsiv-J5aEI/edit#gid=0");
33.   newSS.getActiveSheet().getRange("A1").setValue(text);
34. }
35.
```

```
36.    //Get a value from one spreadsheet and add it into another, using it ID
37.    function example6() {
38.        const text = SHEET.getRange("C1").getValue();
39.        const newSS = SpreadsheetApp.openById("1xFwNEaBjvHeBfxW_z4wBsyozedn5sQ82FWsiv-J5aEI");
40.        newSS.getActiveSheet().getRange("A2").setValue(text);
41.    }
42.
43.    //Create multiple spreadsheets with different names and pieces of text from a sheet
44.    function example7() {
45.        const ssNames = SHEET.getRange("D1:D3").getValues(),
46.            texts = SHEET.getRange("E1:E3").getValues();
47.
48.        for (i in ssNames) {
49.            let spreadsheet = SpreadsheetApp.create(ssNames[i]);
50.            spreadsheet.getActiveSheet().getRange("A1").setValue(texts[i]);
51.        }
52.    }
```

Chapter 7 – Spreadsheet

File: http://bit.ly/3OQy5sb

```
1.  //Copy a spreadsheet, rename the new one using original name
2.  //Display a toast message once the process has finished
3.  function example1() {
4.    const ss1 = SpreadsheetApp.getActiveSpreadsheet(),
5.          ss1Name = ss1.getName();
6.    ss1.copy(ss1Name + "-example1");
7.    ss1.toast("Spreadsheet copied & named", "Finished", 5);
8.  }
9.
10. //Add an editor and viewers to the new spreadsheet
11. function example2() {
12.   const originalSs =
   SpreadsheetApp.openById('1ZI_sgQ3SGbVs4WZwYt6kuMszYFHsngLvtVbnXvvZIwQ'),
13.         ss2 = originalSs.copy("NEW"); //Normally don't include this line
14.   ss2.rename("example2");
15.   ss2.addEditor('brgablog2@gmail.com');
16.   ss2.addViewers(['brgablogse@gmail.com', 'brgablogesp@gmail.com']);
17. }
18.
19. //Move a specific sheet to a new location
20. function example3() {
21.   const currentSs = SpreadsheetApp.getActiveSpreadsheet(),
22.         ss3 = currentSs.copy("example3"),
23.         sheetAll = ss3.getSheetByName("All");
24.   sheetAll.activate();
25.   ss3.moveActiveSheet(5);
26. }
27.
28. //Move a sheet to a new location using getNumSheets
29. function example4() {
30.   const currentSs = SpreadsheetApp.getActiveSpreadsheet(),
31.         ss4 = currentSs.copy("example4"),
32.         sheetAll = ss4.getSheetByName("All");
33.   sheetAll.activate();
34.   const numOfSheets = ss4.getNumSheets();
35.   ss4.moveActiveSheet(numOfSheets);
36. }
37.
38. //Insert a new sheet and delete a sheet
39. function example5() {
40.   const currentSs = SpreadsheetApp.getActiveSpreadsheet(),
41.         ss5 = currentSs.copy("example5"),
42.         numOfSheets = ss5.getNumSheets();
43.   ss5.insertSheet(numOfSheets);
44.   const firstSheet = ss5.getSheets()[0];
45.   ss5.deleteSheet(firstSheet);
46. }
```

Chapter 8 - Sheet

File: http://bit.ly/3rXsrAn

```
1.  //Makes a copy of a hidden master sheet and renames it with the teacher's
    name
2.  function example1() {
3.    const ss = SpreadsheetApp.getActiveSpreadsheet(),
4.      ssId = ss.getId(),
5.      destination = SpreadsheetApp.openById(ssId),
6.      master = ss.getSheetByName("master"),
7.      newSheet = master.copyTo(destination);
8.
9.    newSheet.showSheet();
10.     const teachersName = ss.getSheetByName("name").getRange("A1").getValue();
11.     newSheet.setName(teachersName);
12.     newSheet.getRange("A1").setValue(teachersName);
13. }
14.
15. //Hides certain columns and the header row, and inserts a blank column
16. //Then deletes all the blank rows and columns
17. function example2() {
18.   const ss = SpreadsheetApp.getActiveSpreadsheet(),
19.     classes = ss.getSheetByName("classes");
20.   classes.hideColumns(2);
21.   classes.hideColumns(5, 3);
22.   classes.hideRows(1);
23.   classes.insertColumns(5);
24.
25.   const lastRow = classes.getLastRow(),
26.     maxRow = classes.getMaxRows(),
27.     blankRows = maxRow - lastRow;
28.   if (blankRows > 0) {
29.     classes.deleteRows(lastRow + 1, blankRows);
30.   }
31.
32.   const lastColumn = classes.getLastColumn(),
33.     maxColumn = classes.getMaxColumns(),
34.     blankColumns = maxColumn - lastColumn;
35.   if (blankColumns > 0) {
36.     classes.deleteColumns(lastColumn + 1, blankColumns);
37.   }
38. }
39.
40. //Adds teachers name to a list of teachers on a different sheet
41. //Then adjusts the column width automatically and sorts the list
42. function example3() {
43.   const ss = SpreadsheetApp.getActiveSpreadsheet(),
44.     teachersName = ss.getSheetByName("name").getRange("A1").getValue(),
45.     teachersList = ss.getSheetByName("teachers");
46.   teachersList.appendRow([teachersName]);
47.
48.   teachersList.autoResizeColumn(1);
49.   teachersList.sort(1);
50. }
```

```
51.
52.   //Asks the user for the teacher's row number then makes a new sheet for that teacher with their class details
53.   function example4() {
54.     const ui = SpreadsheetApp.getUi(),
55.       response = ui.prompt('Teacher', 'Which teacher do you want? Enter row number.', ui.ButtonSet.OK_CANCEL);
56.     if (response.getSelectedButton() === ui.Button.OK) {
57.       const rowNumber = response.getResponseText();
58.     }
59.
60.     const ss = SpreadsheetApp.getActiveSpreadsheet(),
61.       classes = ss.getSheetByName("classes"),
62.       teachers = classes.getDataRange().getValues();
63.
64.     const teachersName = teachers[rowNumber - 1][0],
65.       newSheet = ss.insertSheet(teachersName);
66.
67.     const headers = teachers.shift(),
68.       teacherInfo = teachers[rowNumber - 2];
69.
70.     newSheet.appendRow(headers);
71.     newSheet.appendRow(teacherInfo);
72.   }
73.
74.   //The same as example4 but a quicker way
75.   function example5() {
76.     const ui = SpreadsheetApp.getUi(),
77.       response = ui.prompt('Teacher', 'Which teacher do you want? Enter row number.', ui.ButtonSet.OK_CANCEL);
78.     if (response.getSelectedButton() == ui.Button.OK) {
79.       const rowNumber = response.getResponseText();
80.     }
81.
82.     const ss = SpreadsheetApp.getActiveSpreadsheet(),
83.       classes = ss.getSheetByName("classes"),
84.       teachers = classes.getDataRange().getValues();
85.
86.     const teachersName = teachers[rowNumber - 1][0],
87.       newSheet = ss.insertSheet(teachersName);
88.
89.     const headers = teachers.shift(),
90.       teacherInfo = teachers[rowNumber - 2];
91.
92.     const info = [];
93.     info.push(headers);
94.     info.push(teacherInfo);
95.
96.     newSheet.getRange(1, 1, info.length, info[0].length).setValues(info);
97.   }
```

Chapter 9 – Range

File: http://bit.ly/3eKHVUN

```
1.  //EXAMPLE 1 - Open sheet, highlight a certain cell and clear its content
2.  function onOpen() {
3.    const ss = SpreadsheetApp.getActiveSpreadsheet(),
4.        sheet1 = ss.getSheetByName("eg1"),
5.        cell = sheet1.getRange("B4");
6.    cell.activate()
7.      .clearContent();
8.  }
9.
10. //EXAMPLE 2 - Set up onFormSubmit trigger
11. function example2Trigger() {
12.   const ss = SpreadsheetApp.getActiveSpreadsheet();
13.   ScriptApp.newTrigger("example2")
14.     .forSpreadsheet(ss)
15.     .onFormSubmit()
16.     .create();
17. }
18.
19. //EXAMPLE 2 - Add formula to last row, which is triggered when a form is submitted
20. function example2() {
21.   const ss = SpreadsheetApp.getActiveSpreadsheet(),
22.       sheet2 = ss.getSheetByName("eg2"),
23.       lastRow = sheet2.getLastRow();
24.   sheet2.getRange(lastRow, 4).setFormulaR1C1("=R[0]C[-1]-R[0]C[-2]");
25. }
26.
27. //EXAMPLE 3 - Set up onFormSubmit trigger
28. function example3Trigger() {
29.   const ss = SpreadsheetApp.getActiveSpreadsheet();
30.   ScriptApp.newTrigger("example3")
31.     .forSpreadsheet(ss)
32.     .onFormSubmit()
33.     .create();
34. }
35.
36. //EXAMPLE 3 - Add formula, add formatting when a form is submitted
37. function example3() {
38.   const ss = SpreadsheetApp.getActiveSpreadsheet(),
39.       sheet3 = ss.getSheetByName("eg3"),
40.       lastRow = sheet3.getLastRow();
41.
42.   sheet3.getRange(lastRow, 4).setFormulaR1C1("=R[0]C[-1]-R[0]C[-2]");
43.
44.   const times = sheet3.getRange(lastRow, 2, 1, 3);
45.   times.setNumberFormat("HH:mm");
46.
47.   const data = sheet3.getDataRange();
48.   data.setHorizontalAlignment("center")
49.     .setBorder(true, true, true, true, true, true);
50.
```

```
51.      sheet3.getRange(lastRow, 1).setNumberFormat("DD/MM/YYYY");
52.   }
53.
54.   //EXAMPLE4 - Change status to red or green
55.   //NB: This example won't work as the next example also uses onEdit
56.   //Comment out lines 73 to 99, to see this one working
57.   function onEdit(e) {
58.     const sh = SpreadsheetApp.getActiveSheet(),
59.       status = e.value,
60.       range = e.range,
61.       column = range.getColumn(),
62.       row = range.getRow();
63.
64.     if (sh.getName() === "eg4" && column === 3 && row > 1 && row < 6) {
65.       if (status === "Closed") {
66.         range.setBackground("#66BB6A");
67.       }
68.       else if (status === "Open") {
69.         range.setBackground("#EF5350");
70.       }
71.     }
72.   }
73.
74.   //EXAMPLE5 - Change row to red or green depending on status
75.   function onEdit(e) {
76.     const sh = SpreadsheetApp.getActiveSheet(),
77.       status = e.value,
78.       range = e.range,
79.       column = range.getColumn(),
80.       row = range.getRow();
81.
82.     if (sh.getName() === "eg5" && column === 3 && row > 1 && row < 6) {
83.       if (status === "Closed") {
84.         const rowToColor = range.offset(0, -2, 1, 3);
85.         rowToColor.setBackground("#66BB6A");
86.       }
87.
88.       else if (status === "Open") {
89.         const rowToColor = range.offset(0, -2, 1, 3);
90.         rowToColor.setBackground("#EF5350");
91.       }
92.
93.       else {
94.         const rowToColor = range.offset(0, -2, 1, 3);
95.         rowToColor.setBackground("#FFFFFF");
96.       }
97.     }
98.   }
99.
100.  //EXAMPLE 6 - Sort table by average mark and then by student's name
101.  function example6() {
102.    const ss = SpreadsheetApp.getActiveSpreadsheet(),
103.      sheet6 = ss.getSheetByName("eg6"),
104.      range = sheet6.getDataRange();
105.    range.sort([{ column: 4, ascending: false }, { column: 1, ascending: true }]);
106.  }
107.
```

```javascript
//EXAMPLE 7 - Copy part of a table to a new sheet
function example7() {
  const ss = SpreadsheetApp.getActiveSpreadsheet(),
    sheet7 = ss.getSheetByName("eg7"),
    range = sheet7.getRange(1, 1, 13, 3);

  const checkNewSheet = ss.getSheetByName("new");
  if (checkNewSheet) {
    ss.deleteSheet(checkNewSheet);
  }

  const newSheet = ss.insertSheet("new"),
    newSheetRange = newSheet.getRange(1, 1, 13, 3);
  range.copyTo(newSheetRange);

  newSheet.autoResizeColumn(1);
  newSheet.setColumnWidth(3, 400);
  newSheet.getRange(1, 3, 100).setWrap(true);
}
```

Appendix 2 – Files and code from each chapter (Forms)

Chapter 10 – First Form Script

File: http://bit.ly/3s7V1ix

```
1.  function myFunction() {
2.    FormApp.getActiveForm().setTitle("Questionnaire");
3.  }
```

Chapter 11 – Creating & updating a Google Form

File: http://bit.ly/3tIu8lG

Example 1

```
1.  function createForm() {
2.    const form = FormApp.create("New form");
3.    let formQ1 = form.addMultipleChoiceItem();
4.    formQ1.setTitle('Where do you want to go on holiday?');
5.    formQ1.setChoiceValues(['Seville', 'London']);
6.  }
```

Example 2

```
8.   function createFormFromData() {
9.     const ss = SpreadsheetApp.getActiveSpreadsheet().getSheetByName("newQ");
10.    const question = ss.getRange(2, 1).getValue();
11.    const options = ss.getRange(4, 1, 2).getValues();
12.
13.    const form = FormApp.create("New form");
14.    let formQ1 = form.addMultipleChoiceItem();
15.    formQ1.setTitle(question);
16.    formQ1.setChoiceValues(options);
17.  }
```

Example 3

```
19.  function updateFormFromData() {
20.    const ss =
     SpreadsheetApp.getActiveSpreadsheet().getSheetByName("updateQ");
21.    const question = ss.getRange(2, 1).getValue();
22.    const options = ss.getRange(4, 1, 2).getValues();
```

```
23.
24.     const form = FormApp.openById('FILE ID);
25.     const allItems = form.getItems();
26.     let formQ1 = allItems[0].asMultipleChoiceItem();
27.     formQ1.setTitle(question);
28.     formQ1.setChoiceValues(options);
29.  }
```

Chapter 12 – Creating & updating a multiple question Form

File: http://bit.ly/2PbwESK

Example 1

```
1.  function createFormFromData() {
2.    const sh = SpreadsheetApp.getActiveSpreadsheet().getSheetByName("Sheet1");
3.
4.    //Get data, number of questions and options irfo
5.    const data = sh.getDataRange().getValues();
6.    const numOfOptions = data.length-3;
7.    const numOfQs = data[0].length;
8.
9.    //Get questions
10.     const questions = sh.getRange(2, 2, 1, numOfQs).getValues();
11.
12.    //Get options and store in an array
13.    var allOptions = [];
14.    for (q=2;q<=numOfQs;q++){
15.      let options = sh.getRange(3, q, numOfOptions).getValues();
16.      allOptions.push(options);
17.    }
18.
19.    //Create the form
20.    const form = FormApp.create("New forn");
21.
22.    //Add questions and options to form
23.    for (qq=0;qq<numOfQs-1;qq++){
24.      let formQ = form.addMultipleChoiceItem();
25.      formQ.setTitle(questions[0][qq]);
26.      formQ.setChoiceValues(allOptions[qq]);
27.    }
28.  }
```

Example 2

```
30.  function updateFormFromData() {
31.    const sh =
   SpreadsheetApp.getActiveSpreadsheet().getSheetByName("Sheet2");
32.
```

```
33.    //Get data, number of questions and options info
34.    const data = sh.getDataRange().getValues();
35.    const numOfOptions = data.length-3;
36.    const numOfQs = data[0].length;
37.
38.    //Get questions
39.    const questions = sh.getRange(2, 2, 1, numOfQs).getValues();
40.
41.    //Get options and store in an array
42.    var allOptions = [];
43.    for (q=2;q<=numOfQs;q++){
44.      let options = sh.getRange(3, q, numOfOptions).getValues();
45.      allOptions.push(options);
46.    }
47.
48.    //Get existing form
49.    const form = FormApp.openById('FORM ID');
50.    const allItems = form.getItems();
51.
52.    //Add questions and options to form
53.    for (qq=0;qq<numOfQs-1;qq++){
54.      let formQ = allItems[qq].asMultipleChoiceItem();
55.      formQ.setTitle(questions[0][qq]);
56.      formQ.setChoiceValues(allOptions[qq]);
57.    }
58. }
```

Chapter 13 – Adding different types of questions to a Form

File: http://bit.ly/3r3qCAB

```
1.  //Create new form - Global variable so it can be seen by all functions
2.  const FORM = FormApp.create("Questionnaire");
3.
4.  function makeQuestionnaire() {
5.  //Get data and last row from spreadsheet
6.    const sh = SpreadsheetApp.getActiveSpreadsheet().getSheetByName("Sheet1");
7.    const data = sh.getDataRange().getValues();
8.
9.
10.   //Loop through each question and check what question type it is
11.     data.forEach(checkQuestionType)
12.  }
13.
14.   //function to check question type
15.   function checkQuestionType(data){
16.     if(data[1] === "text"){
17.       makeTextQ(data);
18.     }
19.     else if(data[1] === "date"){
20.       makeDateQ(data);
21.     }
```

```
22.      else if(data[1] === "duration"){
23.         makeDurationQ(data);
24.      }
25.      else if(data[1] === "multiplec"){
26.         makeMultipleCQ(data);
27.      }
28.      else if(data[1] === "list"){
29.         makeListQ(data);
30.      }
31.      else if(data[1] === "scale"){
32.         makeScaleQ(data);
33.      }
34.      else if(data[1] === "checkbox"){
35.         makeCheckboxQ(data);
36.      }
37.      else if(data[1] === "grid"){
38.         makeGridQ(data);
39.      }
40.      else if(data[1] === "paragraph"){
41.         makeParagraphQ(data);
42.      }
43. }
44.
45. ////Functions to make different types of questions
46. //Make text question
47. function makeTextQ(data){
48.     let text = data[2];
49.     let item = FORM.addTextItem();
50.     item.setTitle(text);
51. }
52.
53. //Make date question
54. function makeDateQ(data){
55.     let date = data[2];
56.     let item = FORM.addDateItem();
57.     item.setTitle(date);
58.     item.setRequired(true);
59. }
60.
61. //make duration question
62. function makeDurationQ(data){
63.     let duration = data[2];
64.     let item = FORM.addDurationItem();
65.     item.setTitle(duration);
66. }
67.
68. //make Multiple-Choice question
69. function makeMultipleCQ(data){
70.     let mcQuestion = data[2];
71.     let item = FORM.addMultipleChoiceItem();
72.     item.setTitle(mcQuestion);
73.
74.     //Getting options
75.     let trimmedData = data.filter(function(str) {
76.         return /\S/.test(str);
77.     });
78.     //Getting options without spaces
79.     let slicedData = trimmedData.slice(3,trimmedData.length);
```

```
80.
81.    //Adding option to Form
82.    item.setChoiceValues(slicedData);
83.  }
84.
85.  //make List question
86.  function makeListQ(data){
87.    let listQuestion = data[2];
88.    let item = FORM.addListItem();
89.    item.setTitle(listQuestion);
90.    let trimmedData = data.filter(function(str) {
91.      return /\S/.test(str);
92.      });
93.
94.    let slicedData = trimmedData.slice(3,trimmedData.length);
95.    item.setChoiceValues(slicedData);
96.  }
97.
98.  //make Scale question
99.  function makeScaleQ(data){
100.    let scaleQ = data[2];
101.    let item = FORM.addScaleItem();
102.    item.setTitle(scaleQ);
103.
104.    let trimmedData = data.filter(function(str) {
105.    return /\S/.test(str);
106.    });
107.
108.    //Get and set lower and upper bounds of scale
109.    let lower = trimmedData.slice(3, 4);
110.    let upper = trimmedData.slice(4, 5);
111.    item.setBounds(lower, upper);
112.    //Set labels to lower and upper bounds
113.    item.setLabels(trimmedData.slice(5, 6), trimmedData.slice(6, 7));
114.  }
115.
116. //make Checkbox question
117. function makeCheckboxQ(data){
118.    let checkboxQ = data[2];
119.    let item = FORM.addCheckboxItem();
120.    item.setTitle(checkboxQ);
121.    let trimmedData = data.filter(function(str) {
122.      return /\S/.test(str);
123.      });
124.    let slicedData = trimmedData.slice(3,trimmedData.length);
125.     item.setChoiceValues(slicedData);
126. }
127.
128. //make Grid question
129. function makeGridQ(data){
130.    let gridQ = data[2];
131.    let item = FORM.addGridItem();
132.    item.setTitle(gridQ);
133.
134.    let trimmedData = data.filter(function(str) {
135.      return /\S/.test(str);
136.      });
137.
```

```
138.    //Find where "Columns:" text is in array
139.    let columnPosition = trimmedData.indexOf("Columns:");
140.
141.    //Get row values for grid
142.    let slicedDataRows = trimmedData.slice(3,columnPosition);
143.    //Get column values for grid
144.    let slicedDataColumns =
     trimmedData.slice(columnPosition+1,trimmedData.length);
145.
146.    item.setRows(slicedDataRows);
147.    item.setColumns(slicedDataColumns);
148. }
149.
150. //make Paragraph question
151. function makeParagraphQ(data){
152.    let paragraphText = data[2];
153.    let item = FORM.addParagraphTextItem();
154.    item.setTitle(paragraphText);
155. }
```

Chapter 14 – Using Form responses

Below are the links to the files and the full pieces of code for each example.

Example 1 - Problem log

Files

Sheet: http://bit.ly/3cMvOni

Form: http://bit.ly/3sl32Al

Sheet version

```
1.  function sendProblem() {
2.    const ss = SpreadsheetApp.getActiveSpreadsheet(),
3.      fr = ss.getSheetByName("Form Responses 1"),
4.      lastRowValues = fr.getRange(fr.getLastRow(), 1, 1,
    fr.getLastColumn()).getValues(),
5.      problem = lastRowValues[0][1],
6.      room = lastRowValues[0][2];
7.
8.    //Create email
9.    const emailSubject = "Problem",
10.       emailTo = 'brgablog@gmail.com, brgablog2@gmail.com',
11.       emailBody = "Problem: " + problem + "<br /> \
12.   Room: " + room;
13.
```

```
14.    //Send email
15.    MailApp.sendEmail(emailTo, emailSubject, '', {
16.      htmlBody: emailBody
17.    });
18.  }
```

Form version

```
1.  function sendProblemFromForm() {
2.    //Get submitted problem and room from form
3.    const form = FormApp.getActiveForm(),
4.      formResponses = form.getResponses(),
5.      latestFR = formResponses[form.getResponses().length - 1];
6.
7.    const itemResponses = latestFR.getItemResponses(),
8.      problem = itemResponses[0].getResponse(),
9.      room = itemResponses[1].getResponse();
10.
11.    //Create email
12.    const emailSubject = "Problem",
13.      emailTo = 'brgablog@gmail.com, brgablog2@gmail.com',
14.      emailBody = "Problem: " + problem + "<br /> \
15.    Room: " + room;
16.
17.    //Send email
18.    MailApp.sendEmail(emailTo, emailSubject, '', {
19.      htmlBody: emailBody
20.    });
21.  }
```

Example 2 - Assignments

Files

Sheet: http://bit.ly/3lBWtY1

Form: http://bit.ly/38Z1qVF

```
1.  function assignments() {
2.    const ss = SpreadsheetApp.getActiveSpreadsheet();
3.
4.  //Get assignment
5.    const fr = ss.getSheetByName("Assignment1");
6.    const lastRowValues = fr.getRange(fr.getLastRow(), 1, 1, fr.getLastColumn()).getValues();
7.
8.  //Get the sheet of the student who's just submitted and append their assignment on that sheet
9.    const sheets = ss.getSheets();
10.     for (var sh = 0 ; sh < sheets.length ; sh++) {
11.      let sheetName = sheets[sh].getSheetName();
12.      if(lastRowValues[0][1] === sheetName){
```

```
13.         ss.getSheetByName(sheetName).appendRow(lastRowValues[0]);
14.       }
15.     }
16. }
```

Example 3 - Appointments

File (Form): http://bit.ly/316IcZY

```
1.  function meetingTimes() {
2.    const form = FormApp.getActiveForm();
3.
4.  //Get current times on Form
5.    let timesArray = [];
6.    const questions = form.getItems();
7.    const timeQ = questions[1].asMultipleChoiceItem();
8.    const choices = timeQ.getChoices();
9.    for (var i = 0; i < choices.length; i++) {
10.      timesArray.push(choices[i].getValue());
11.   }
12.
13.  //Get all form responses and the latest one
14.    const formResponses = form.getResponses();
15.    const latestFR = formResponses[form.getResponses().length-1];
16.
17.  //Get submitted time from form
18.    const itemResponses = latestFR.getItemResponses();
19.    const itemResponse = itemResponses[1];
20.    const submittedTime = itemResponse.getResponse();
21.
22.  //Remove submittedTime from array
23.    for (x in timesArray){
24.     if(timesArray[x] === submittedTime) {
25.      const indexT = timesArray.indexOf(submittedTime);
26.      timesArray.splice(indexT, 1);
27.     }
28.    }
29.
30.  //Replace time question on form with array
31.    timeQ.setChoiceValues(timesArray);
32. }
```

```
1. function setUpForm() {
2.   const form = FormApp.getActiveForm();
3.   const questions = form.getItems();
4.   const timeQ = questions[1].asMultipleChoiceItem();
5.
   timeQ.setChoiceValues(['09:00','09:30','10:00','10:30','11:00','11:30','12:00']);
6. }
```

Chapter 15 - Form validation

File: http://bit.ly/3lFeKnA

```
1.  function setUpValidation() {
2.    //Set up form
3.    const form = FormApp.create('Clocking in');
4.    form.setTitle('Clocking in form');
5.
6.    //Set up page
7.    const item = form.addTextItem()
8.      .setTitle('Employee Number')
9.      .setRequired(true);
10.
11.   const textVal = FormApp.createTextValidation()
12.     .setHelpText("Enter your 4 digit employee number.")
13.     .requireNumberEqualTo(1234)
14.     .build();
15.   item.setValidation(textVal);
16.
17.   form.addMultipleChoiceItem()
18.     .setTitle('Clocking in or out?')
19.     .setChoiceValues(["Clock in", "Clock out"])
20.     .setRequired(true);
21. }
```

Chapter 16 – Form page navigation

File: http://bit.ly/2NJjrjG

```
1.  function setUpForm() { //Clocking in form v2
2.    //Set up form
3.    const form = FormApp.create('Clocking in v2');
4.    form.setTitle('Clocking in form');
5.
6.    //Set up first page
7.    const item1 = form.addListItem()
8.      .setTitle('Employee Name')
9.      .setRequired(true);
10.
11.   const page2 = form.addPageBreakItem()
12.     .setTitle('Fred');
13.
14.   //Set up second page (Fred)
15.   const item2 = form.addTextItem()
16.     .setTitle('Employee Number')
```

```
17.            .setRequired(true);
18.
19.       const textVal2 = FormApp.createTextValidation()
20.            .setHelpText("Enter your 4 digit employee number.")
21.            .requireNumberEqualTo(1234)
22.            .build();
23.       item2.setValidation(textVal2);
24.
25.       form.addMultipleChoiceItem()
26.            .setTitle('Clocking in or out?')
27.            .setChoiceValues(["Clock in", "Clock out"])
28.            .setRequired(true);
29.
30.       const page3 = form.addPageBreakItem()
31.            .setTitle('Wilma')
32.            .setGoToPage(FormApp.PageNavigationType.SUBMIT);
33.
34.       //Set up third page (Wilma)
35.       const item3 = form.addTextItem()
36.            .setTitle('Employee Number')
37.            .setRequired(true);
38.
39.       const textVal3 = FormApp.createTextValidation()
40.            .setHelpText("Enter your 4 digit employee number.")
41.            .requireNumberEqualTo(3456)
42.            .build();
43.       item3.setValidation(textVal3);
44.
45.       form.addMultipleChoiceItem()
46.            .setTitle('Clocking in or out?')
47.            .setChoiceValues(["Clock in", "Clock out"])
48.            .setRequired(true);
49.
50.       const page4 = form.addPageBreakItem()
51.            .setTitle('Betty')
52.            .setGoToPage(FormApp.PageNavigationType.SUBMIT);
53.
54.       //Set up forth page (Betty)
55.       const item4 = form.addTextItem()
56.            .setTitle('Employee Number')
57.            .setRequired(true);
58.
59.       var textVal4 = FormApp.createTextValidation()
60.            .setHelpText("Enter your 4 digit employee number.")
61.            .requireNumberEqualTo(6789)
62.            .build();
63.       item4.setValidation(textVal4);
64.
65.       form.addMultipleChoiceItem()
66.            .setTitle('Clocking in or out?')
67.            .setChoiceValues(["Clock in", "Clock out"])
68.            .setRequired(true);
69.
70.       //Set up name choices on first page
71.       item1.setChoices([
72.         item1.createChoice("Fred", page2),
73.         item1.createChoice("Wilma", page3),
74.         item1.createChoice("Betty", page4)
```

```
75.    ]);
76. }
```

Chapter 17 – Making quizzes in Google Forms

File: http://bit.ly/3r8ylrU (code in Form Script editor)

```
1.  function createGradedCheckboxQuestionWithAutofeedback() {
2.    // Make sure the form is a quiz.
3.    const form = FormApp.create("Quiz");
4.    form.setIsQuiz(true);
5.
6.    // Make a 10 point question and set up the question
7.    const item = form.addCheckboxItem();
8.    item.setTitle("What flavors are in neapolitan ice cream?");
9.    item.setPoints(10);
10.
11.   // chocolate, vanilla, & strawberry are the correct answers
12.   item.setChoices([
13.     item.createChoice("chocolate", true),
14.     item.createChoice("vanilla", true),
15.     item.createChoice("rum raisin", false),
16.     item.createChoice("strawberry", true),
17.     item.createChoice("mint", false)
18.   ]);
19.
20.   // If the respondent answers correctly,
21.   // they'll see this feedback when they viewscores.
22.   const correctFeedback = FormApp.createFeedback()
23.       .setText("You're an ice cream expert!")
24.       .build();
25.   item.setFeedbackForCorrect(correctFeedback);
26.
27.   // If they respond incorrectly, they'll see this feedback with
28.   // helpful link to read more about ice cream.
29.   const incorrectFeedback = FormApp.createFeedback()
30.       .setText("Sorry, wrong answer")
31.       .addLink(
32.         "https://en.wikipedia.org/wiki/Neapolitan_ice_cream",
33.         "Read more")
34.       .build();
35.   item.setFeedbackForIncorrect(incorrectFeedback);
36. }
```

Appendix 3 – Script Editor and creating a standalone script

Here, let's look at the Script Editor in more detail. Open it up from the Tools menu.

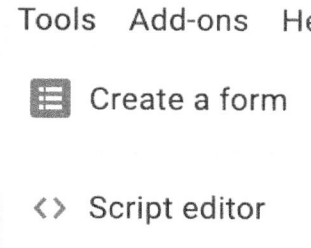

Tour of the Script editor

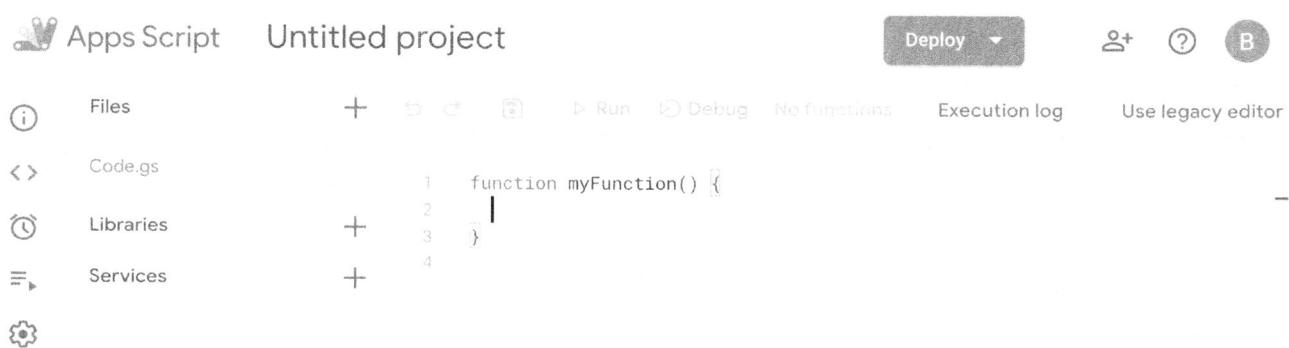

Usually when I open a new script project, I rename it straight away, to avoid having lots of Untitled projects. Just click on "Untitled project" and give it a name.

By default, it opens in the Code section of the editor where you'll spend most of your time, but there are other parts to it too. On the left-hand side, you'll see 5 icons.

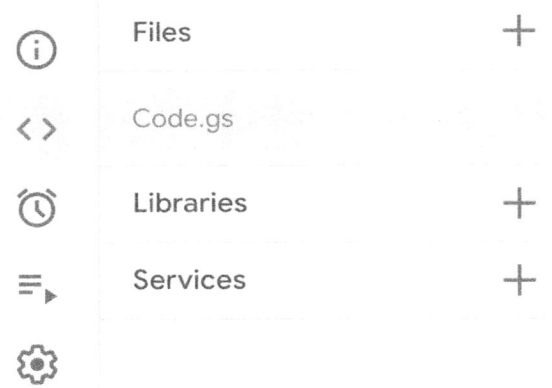

Hover over the icons and you'll see their descriptions appear. Let's look at these one-by-one.

Overview

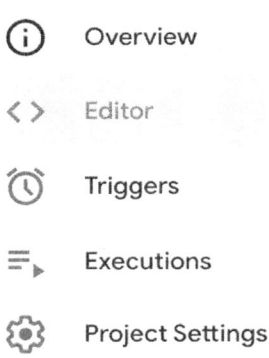

Click on "Overview". This gives you information on the script project as a whole.

Project Details

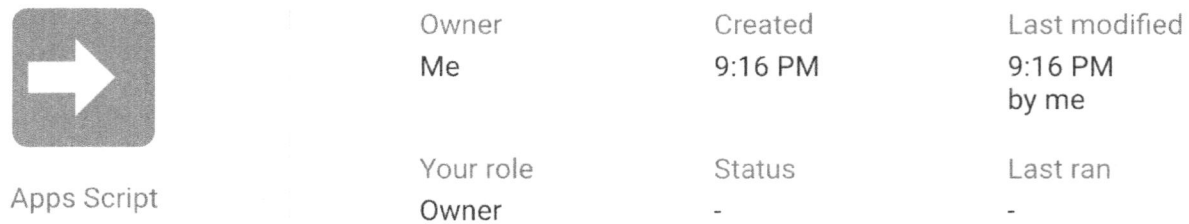

It will give you information on the executions and any errors.

Deployments

All   Head

7 Day Summary

Error rate	Executions	Users
0%	0	0
% of executions w/ errors	# of times your scripts ran	# of users for your script

It will even tell you when those errors happened in the form of a graph.

Health

Editor

Along the top of the editor you have the toolbar.

↶ ↷ 💾 ▷ Run ⏵ Debug myFunction ▼ Execution log

Going from left to right we have:

Undo, redo

Save (the project)

Run (the function)

Debug – Find where there are problems in your code.

myFunction – This is where you 'll have a list of the functions in that particular script file.

Execution log – This will open the execution log and show the last program executed with any logs registered.

Helpful Editor tools

The editor is full of tools to make your coding life easier. Below are some of the most useful ones, especially for beginners.

Formatting (indenting) your document

When you type in your code, you should indent sections of the code to make it easier to read. This is not always obvious to a beginner, and even to someone more experienced, manually indenting your code can be time-consuming, so fortunately, there's a shortcut.

Below is code that hasn't been indented:

```
function onOpen() {
const ss = SpreadsheetApp.getActiveSpreadsheet(),
sheet1 = ss.getSheetByName("eg1"),
cell = sheet1.getRange("B4");
cell.activate()
.clearContent();
}
```

Right-click somewhere in the code and you'll see a menu. Click on "Format document" (or you can use the keyboard shortcut that is shown.

Format Document   ⇧⌥F

This will correctly indent your whole script file. For example, you can see the function is on one level, then the constant on another, and the additional constants, on another.

```
2   function onOpen() {
3     const ss = SpreadsheetApp.getActiveSpreadsheet(),
4       sheet1 = ss.getSheetByName("eg1"),
5       cell = sheet1.getRange("B4");
6     cell.activate()
7       .clearContent();
8   }
```

Highlighting all positions of a variable

When you click on a variable, such as *ss*, it will highlight other instances of that variable, which can help you find where it's being used.

```
const ss = SpreadsheetApp.get
  sheet1 = ss.getSheetByName(
```

Highlighting pairs of brackets

In longer code with multiple brackets, it's sometimes difficult to see the chunk of code contained in a pair of brackets, so it's useful to find the bracket pairs. Plus, it's a way to check the brackets are being paired correctly. Click on one and the paired bracket will be highlighted.

```
function onOpen() {
  const ss = Spreads
    sheet1 = ss.getS
    cell = sheet1.ge
  cell.activate()
    .clearContent();
}
```

Hiding blocks of code

You will notice the downward arrows on the left-hand side of the code. These highlight blocks of code. Sometimes in longer code, it's useful to hide certain ones, to make it easier to concentrate on certain blocks. To hide a block of code, click on the downward arrow next to it.

```
2 ∨  function onOpen() {
3 ∨      const ss = SpreadsheetApp.getActiveS|
4            sheet1 = ss.getSheetByName("eg1"),
5            cell = sheet1.getRange("B4");
6 ∨      cell.activate()
7            .clearContent();
```

As you can see this has hidden lines 4 and 5 which are connected to line 4.

```
2 ∨  function onOpen() {
3 >      const ss = Spreads
6 ∨      cell.activate()
7            .clearContent();
```

Find where a variable is defined

You can quickly find where a variable is defined by right-clicking on the variable and selecting Go to definition.

| Go to Definition | ⌘F12 |

This will take you to the line where that variable is defined.

```
const ss = SpreadsheetApp.getActiveSpreadsheet(),
```

Triggers

We'll come back to the editor, let's now look at the Triggers section.

- ⓘ Overview
- <> Editor
- ⏰ Triggers
- ≡▸ Executions
- ⚙ Project Settings

This is where it lists all the triggers for the project, which run certain functions automatically based on criteria you set up, either manually or in a script.

To add a new trigger manually, click on Add trigger.

To set one up you need to define certain criteria:

The function to be run, the type of deployment…

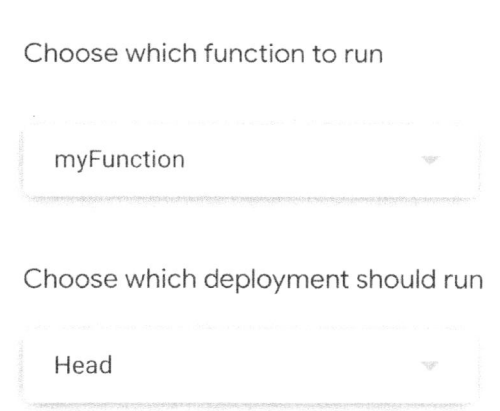

what type of trigger it will be (which could be from an event on the spreadsheet, time-based, or calendar-based), the time interval or an event like a form submission, and if it's time-based how often this should happen.

Select event source

Time-driven

Select type of time based trigger

Hour timer

Select hour interval

Every hour

On the right-hand side, you can set up receiving emails if your trigger fails.

Failure notification settings +

Notify me daily

Here we have an example trigger set up.

Owned by	Last run	Deployment	Event	Function	Error rate
Me	-	Head	Time-based	myFunction	-

Executions

- Overview
- Editor
- Triggers
- Executions
- Project Settings

Next we have Executions which will register every time your script is run, with how it was run, how long it took, and if it completed or failed.

Deployment	Function	Type	Start Time	Duration	Status
Head	myFunction	Editor	Mar 15, 2021, 9:21:08 PM	0.368 s	Completed

Showing 1 execution over last 7 days | Show

Project settings

- Overview
- Editor
- Triggers
- Executions
- Project Settings

Finally, we have the project settings. As a beginner, you're unlikely to need the information in here.

Project Settings

General settings

Settings that pertain to the entire Apps Script project. Changes to these settings will not impact your existing deployment.

- ☑ Log uncaught exceptions to Cloud logs
- ☑ Enable Chrome V8 runtime
- ☐ Show "appsscript.json" manifest file in editor

IDs

IDs are the unique identifiers of your Apps Script project.

Script ID   1ODHW6q4nNXUQNtkvXJpLWCeygtZRxI8EHGEsm3ujM7oMZg2ZDBdSRoJC
             Copy

Sharing and help

In the top-right-hand corner you have the option to share your script file, if you're collaborating with someone, by clicking on the person icon.

Plus, clicking on the question mark, there are links to the documentation, training, the latest updates to Apps Script, and sending feedback if you encounter any problems with the editor or Apps Script.

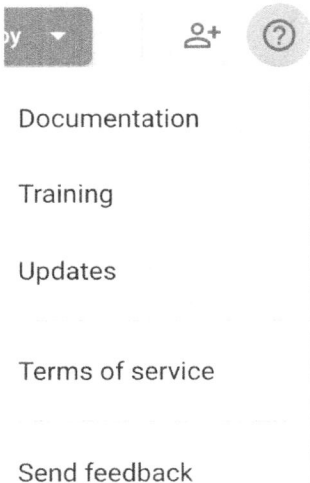

Files, Libraries, and Services

On the left-hand side you can add a new script or HTML file to your project. As I showed in an earlier chapter, you can have multiple files in a single script project.

258

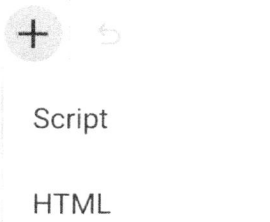

Script

HTML

By clicking on the 3 dots next to the script file, we can rename it, make a copy, and delete it. Plus, we can move them up or down the list. Unfortunately, at the time of writing, there's no way to automatically sort the files by name, like you could do in the old editor.

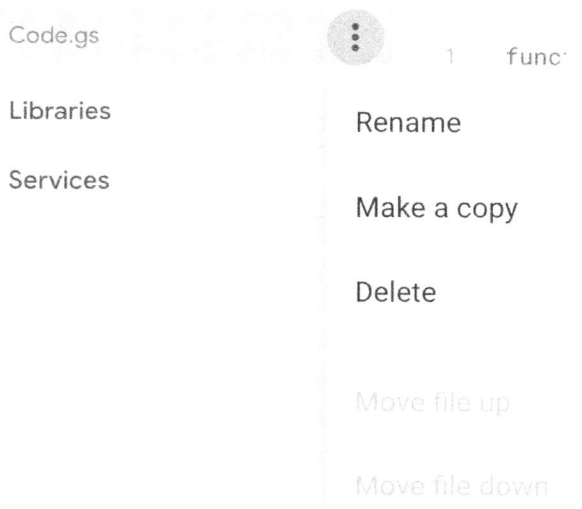

It's possible to connect to other script projects under Libraries. I use this a lot when I have lots of different spreadsheets all using the same code, so rather than having lots of copies of the same script file, I link each one to a master library.

You can also connect to further Workspace Services, e.g. Calendar.

Libraries   +

Services   +

Creating a standalone Apps Script file

All the examples in this book run Apps Script from the Script Editor within Google Sheets and they are called "container-bound scripts", i.e. they live in a file like Sheets. You can however, run scripts from their own Apps Script file.

To do this, you first need to make sure you can create Apps Script files in Google Drive. Click on the New button in Drive and then "More".

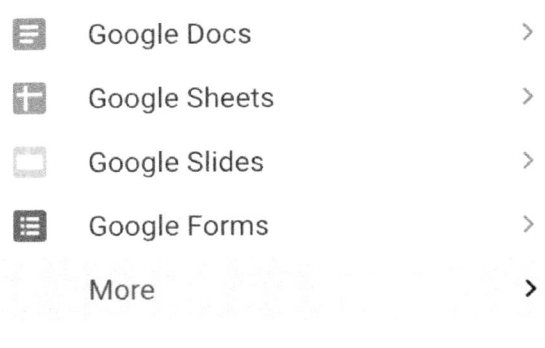

This will show extra apps. Click on google Apps Script to open the Script Editor.

You can write your script from here and instead of saving within a Sheet or Form, the script file is stored as a file on your Google Drive.

This has some advantages:

1) You can save a backup copy of your scripts as an Apps Script file.
2) You can save chunks of code that you often use. For example, below are some of the chunks I use, which saves me time when writing a program. I just open the file and copy and paste the code into the program I'm working on.
3) You can connect different files which use the same script to one central script file via a library.
4) Scripts can be run without using Sheets, Forms, etc, via Web Apps.

- create calendar event
- create Folder & get URL
- Create onFormSubmit trigger
- create random code
- Create random code name
- create Shortcut
- Create Sidebar
- CSV - Import CSV file and remove accents

I recommend backing up your programs as you don't want to lose all that hard work by accidently deleted a file. Plus, having a set up code chunks can speed up your program writing.

Printed in Great Britain
by Amazon